An Adventure With Children

Mary H. Lewis

Edited with an Introduction by
Eugene F. Provenzo, Jr., University of Miami
Therese M. Provenzo, The Park School of Buffalo

University Press of America
Lanham, New York, London

New Introduction Copyright © 1985 by

University Press of America,® Inc.

4720 Boston Way
Lanham, MD 20706

3 Henrietta Street
London WC2E 8LU England

Printed in the United States of America

Originally published by Macmillan Co. in 1928

Library of Congress Cataloging in Publication Data

Lewis, Mary H. (Mary Hammett)
An adventure with children.

  Reprint. Originally published: New York : Macmillan,
1928.
  Bibliography: p.
  1. Park School of Buffalo—History. 2. Lewis,
Mary H. (Mary Hammett) 3. Teachers—New York (State)—
Biography. 4. Open-air schools—New York (State)—
Buffalo—Case studies. 5. Learning by discovery—Case
studies. I. Provenzo, Eugene F. II. Provenzo,
Therese M. III. Title.
LD7501.B86P42   1985   371'.04'09747   85-15821
ISBN 0-8191-4911-X (alk. paper)
ISBN 0-8191-4912-8 (pbk. : alk. paper)

UNIVERSITY
PRESS OF
AMERICA

Mary H. Lewis and a student

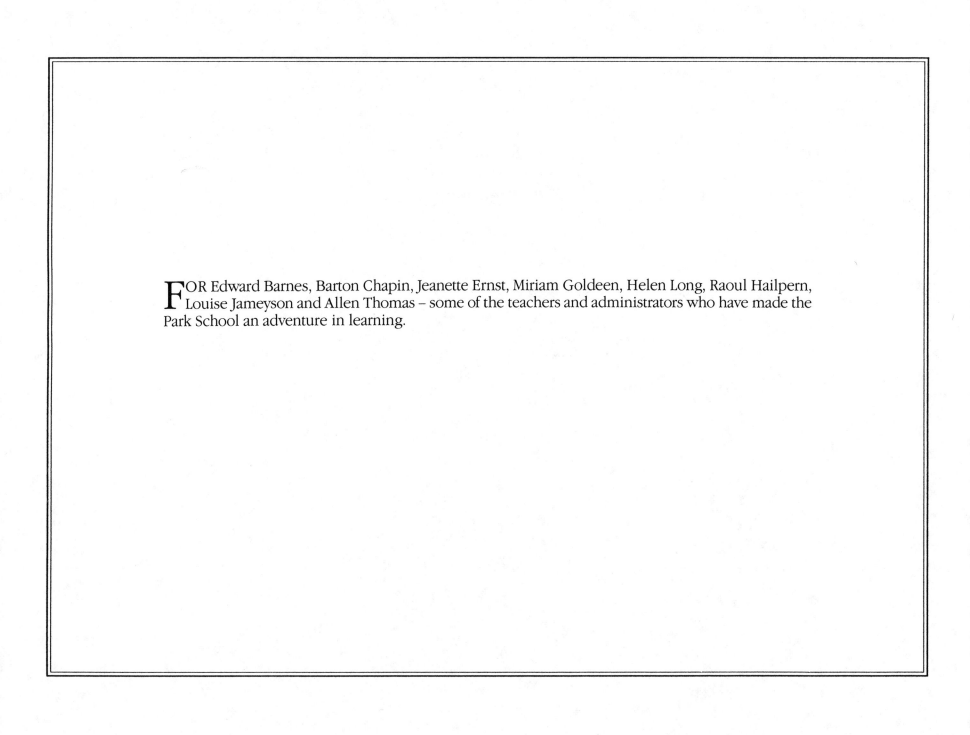

FOR Edward Barnes, Barton Chapin, Jeanette Ernst, Miriam Goldeen, Helen Long, Raoul Hailpern, Louise Jameyson and Allen Thomas – some of the teachers and administrators who have made the Park School an adventure in learning.

Acknowledgements

THE editors wish to thank the many people who have made possible this new edition of Mary H. Lewis's *An Adventure with Children*. Mrs. Stockton Kimball was kind enough to provide a copy of the work from which this reprint has been made. David Hursty, Park School's current headmaster, made available research materials and photographs that have been incorporated into the introduction of this edition. We wish also to thank James E. Lyons of the University Press of America for providing an outlet for the republication of Lewis's work and other documents and sources in the history of American schooling. Special thanks go to Eugene F. Provenzo, Sr. and Asterie Baker Provenzo for their interest and support which has made this project possible.

Eugene F. Provenzo, Jr.
Therese M. Provenzo
Winter, 1984

GROUP DEVELOPMENT
FOR THE
PRIMARY GRADES
THE PARK SCHOOL
AT SNYDER ~ N.Y.

BLEY & LYMAN
ARCHITECTS
250 DELAWARE AVE
BUFFALO N.Y.

Preface

"PARK School is a healthy environment for children." That comment was made recently by a parent who went on to define that environment as physical, academic and psychological. Mary Hammett Lewis would have been pleased to hear that after nearly three-quarters of a century, her ideals, her "adventure with children," continues. Obviously institutions change and evolve, but Park School's roots in the tradition of Progressive education and its basic attitudes toward learning and living are still clearly in evidence at the school.

Education is increasingly in danger of becoming institutionalized and standardized. If she were alive today, Mary Hammett Lewis would undoubtedly stand tall in her support of humanity in the learning environment. Her ideals are more needed today than ever before. Her belief in the essential goodness of children should be the cornerstone for our educational system. Mary Hammett Lewis's adventure should remain a model for us all.

David N. Hursty
Headmaster
The Park School of Buffalo

· SIXTH GRADE · PARK SCHOOL - SNYDER, N.Y.

BLEY & LYMAN, ARCHTS
250 DELAWARE AVE BUFFALO NY

Introduction

IN January of 1896, the American philosopher and educator John Dewey undertook what was to become one of the most important experiments in the history of American education. In a small house near the University of Chicago, Dewey began an experimental or "laboratory" school under the sponsorship of the university's Department of Pedagogy.[1]

The school enrolled a total of 12 children. A contemporary account of its opening described how: "The building, No. 389 Fifty-seventh Street, is a new house; has large windows, sunny rooms and is surrounded by a playground. The work of the first morning began with a song, followed by a survey of the premises to test the knowledge of the children regarding the use of garden, kitchen, etc., as well as their powers of observations. At the end of the morning each child had completed a paper box for pencils and other materials. A story was told by one of the children, and physical exercise concluded the program."[2]

By 1902, the school had grown to a total of 140 students with 23 instructors.[3] More important, the school had pioneered what was undoubtedly the most innovative educational curriculum of the period – one that has continued to shape and influence the course of American education even into our own era. The University Elementary School, or as it has come to be more widely known, the Laboratory School, was the basic testing ground for Dewey's ideas as educator and philosopher. It was through the school that he tested his theories of education and schooling and that the Progressive Education Movement in the United States was begun. For Dewey, the school was literally a pedagogical laboratory. As he explained: "The conception underlying the school is that of a laboratory. It bears the same relation to work in pedagogy that a laboratory bears to biology, physics, or chemistry. Like any such laboratory, it has two main purposes: (1) to exhibit, test, verify, and criticize theoretical statements and principles; (2) to add to the sum of facts and principles in its special line."[4]

Dewey saw traditional methods of education as being inadequate for the rapidly changing and complex society that was emerging in the United States by the end of the nineteenth century. Strongly influenced by the German

Herbartian movement, Dewey and his staff at the Laboratory School developed a curriculum that emphasized the interrelatedness of subjects and the need for children to "learn by doing."[5]

In Dewey's curriculum, the study of a practical art like cooking would lead the child to discover the related sciences of chemistry and botany. The preparation of a Thanksgiving celebration led to history lessons about the Pilgrims, scientific experiments concerning the preservation and storage of food, discussions about the importance of sharing, and vocabulary and writing lessons drawn from their work.[6]

Dewey strongly emphasized the idea of the school as a social environment – a place where children learned and lived out their day-to-day lives. He felt that education was more than a matter of memorizing the "Three Rs," but also involved learning responsibility, sharing in a communal life, and making the first important steps towards independence and adulthood.

Dewey resigned from the University of Chicago in 1904. A short time later he accepted a post on the faculty of Columbia University. Although his appointment at Columbia was in Philosophy, he continued his work in education, maintaining a close affiliation with Teachers College, Columbia University. Dewey soon became enormously influential with both students and faculty at Teachers College.

One individual who was profoundly influenced by Dewey's ideas at Teachers College was Mary Hammett Lewis. Lewis came to New York from Cleveland to teach at the Horace Mann School, then among the most progressive and modern schools in the United States. Horace Mann, affiliated with Teachers College, was intended to provide a testing ground for new pedagogical theories and ideas. Yet despite the wealth of new ideas, more than adequate funding and a highly competent staff, Lewis felt that the school and other schools across the country were somehow failing to meet the needs of children. As she explained in *An Adventure with Children*: "...There had been growing upon me a firm conviction that something was radically wrong with schools everywhere. All my life I had played with children and found them inventive, imaginative, full of ideas, with never quite enough time to carry them out. Yet here in this school, a leader in the schools in this country, we felt stifled, suffocated, when we tried to play, and as for teaching these children I know now that I never did anything which was more futile."[7]

In time, Lewis developed an approach to teaching that was highly personalized and emphasized the interests of the children. Abandoning the formal rigid desks and chairs in her class-

iii

Outdoor classes at the Jewett Avenue location

room, she asked her principal for a large rug where the students could sit as they learned. The rug became a "magic carpet," transforming the classroom and the whole process of teaching and learning. "The attitudes of the children changed completely the moment they set foot on that rug. Language lessons became confidential chats about all sorts of experiences. One day the rug became early Manhattan Island; another day it was the boat of Hendrick Hudson. Unconsciously it began to dawn upon me that the thing I wanted to do was to break up as far as possible the formality and artificiality of my classroom."[8]

The following year the experiment went even further. A tent was pitched on the roof of one of the college buildings. There, eight stories above the ground, overlooking Morningside Heights and Harlem in the distance, Lewis conducted her classes.

Lewis's experiment in open-air education was by no means unique. Open-air education had been introduced from Europe several years before. Intended to help children with respiratory ailments – in particular tuberculosis – the outdoor classes were extremely successful. During the years just prior to the beginning of the First World War the open-air movement achieved widespread popularity throughout the United States.[9]

Lewis's efforts, however, went considerably beyond the philosophy of the open-air movement. Instead she embraced in her work a unique combination of pedagogical theories and ideas. Dewey's progressive educational philosophy, and his emphasis upon the child learning things that were meaningful to his or her own life, were incorporated into Lewis's work. Equally important was the idea of the child as a discoverer and a shaper of things and ideas. As Lewis explained about the children in her rooftop experiment: "They learned to love work because they could see its real significance. They had to be ingenious because the poverty of their equipment demanded it; the simplicity and naturalness of their surroundings made them their best children-selves; and they throve in that atmosphere of freedom and opportunity."[10]

In the spring of 1911, Dewey was contacted by a group of parents who were interested in establishing a progressive school in Buffalo, New York. The group was led by Mrs. Henry Bull. She and other parents had become dissatisfied with the education provided by both the public and private schools in Buffalo. Dewey wrote back, suggesting that a delegation of parents be sent to New York to observe Lewis's rooftop classroom in action.

Nina Bull and Maulsby Kimball led a group

V

Students in costume for a performance of Shakespeare's
"A Midsummer Night's Dream"

of parents to New York to observe Lewis. Remembering them, Lewis said: "I was almost immediately struck with the fact that here were visitors of a different type from those I had been used to seeing. They were not in the least interested in the teacher and her plan of work. They were fascinated by the children and their activities."[11] Lewis agreed to come to Buffalo to set up the proposed school. In 1912 the Park School opened in a small rented cottage on Bird Avenue. Four teachers taught twenty-seven children between three and a half and twelve years of age. Open-air porches were added at the back of each floor of the building.

The following year, the school moved to a large colonial house at Main and Jewett Avenue. Five additional bungalows were built for the school, which included boys through the sixth grade and girls through the eighth grade. In 1920 an Upper School was begun for girls and a 60-acre farm in the suburb of Snyder was purchased from the Hamlin family to house the school. The farm was an ideal location for the school. It included a large and friendly estate house, as well as barns, several cottages and outbuildings. A primary village was added to the new location the following year.[12]

During the Lewis era the school was visited by educators from around the world. Dewey spent a day with the children at the school – an event charmingly recalled by Lewis.[13] Despite Lewis's arguments to the contrary, the number of visitors must have gotten somewhat out of hand. By 1917 the school was averaging six visitors a day. As Lewis recalled: "Teachers and principals and superintendents from almost every large city in the country came to us. One morning we had an M.P. from England, two physicians from Austria, two Japanese students from Columbia University, the president of a great college, a superintendent of schools from the Middle West, and a Harvard professor. . . ."[14]

Among the most interesting early visitors to the school was the writer Dorothy Canfield Fisher, who visited the school at the Jewett Avenue location in 1915. More than anything she was impressed by how the children helped to run the school. As she explained: ". . . In an ultramodern city, I stood in the midst of an old, old-fashioned home, where every process was open to the child's eye, where he took part in all that goes to make a home, where, above all, there was not a button to be pressed. And this old, old-fashioned home called itself the very latest thing in schools! With twentieth-century precision and accuracy it had analyzed the ideal of the old home and it had reconstructed everything in it of value to children."[15] Canfield Fisher saw the

Mary H. Lewis teaching students at the Snyder campus

school and its philosophy as having evolved out of Lewis's "inner consciousness and the spirit of the times."[16] According to her, the natural surroundings provided by the school were the key to its curriculum. Discipline took care of itself in an environment where children were excited about learning and sharing in a communal life.[17]

Lewis was concerned with creating in the Park School an environment in which children might live and grow and flourish, "a place in which a child's soul and mind might be at peace."[18]

The school was her philosophy of education in action. Sadly, problems with the school's board of trustees, evidently over financial management and possibly over differences in educational philosophy, resulted in Lewis's leaving the school in 1925. It marked the end of an era. Other gifted headmasters and teachers would eventually leave their mark on Park School. Yet it is the Lewis years that are of greatest interest to the educational historian and those concerned with the origins of the Progressive Education Movement in America. The reprint that follows of Mary Hammett Lewis's *An Adventure with Children* is intended to once again bring alive the story of an important pioneering experiment in education and the love and concern of a gifted teacher in helping children find meaning in their lives.

Footnotes

1. For background on Dewey and his work as an educator see Arthur G. Wirth, *John Dewey as Educator: His Design for Work in Education (1894-1904)* (New York: John Wiley & Sons, 1966) and George Dykhuizen, *The Life and Mind of John Dewey* (Carbondale, Illinois: Southern Illinois University Press, 1973). The history of Dewey's work at the Laboratory School is found in Katherine Camp Mayhew and Anna Camp Edwards, *The Dewey School* (New York: Appleton-Century Co., 1936), and Ida B. DePencier, *The History of the Laboratory Schools* (Chicago: Quadrangle Books, 1967). Dewey outlined his ideas concerning education in numerous articles and books throughout his career. His most important single work on the subject was *Democracy and Education* (New York: Macmillan, 1916). Those interested in obtaining a general background on Dewey's concerns as an educator during the period when the Laboratory School was getting under way should read his *School and Society* (Chicago: University of Chicago Press, 1900) and *The Child and the Curriculum* (Chicago: University of Chicago Press, 1902).

2. "The Model School," *University of Chicago Weekly*, Vol. 16, January 1896, p. 707.

3. *Dykhuizen*, p. 88.

4. John Dewey, "The University School," *University Record*, Vol. 1, November 6, 1896, p. 417.

5. For background on the impact of Herbart in the United States see: Charles E. Strickland, "The Child, the Community and Clio: The Uses of Cultural History in Elementary School Experiments of the Eighteen-Nineties," *History of Education Quarterly*, Vol. 7, Winter 1967, pp. 474-92.

6. Background on how the various curriculums functioned at the Laboratory School is included in: Wirth, *op. cit.* A detailed discussion of the history curriculum is included in Eugene F. Provenzo, Jr., "History as Experiment: The Role of the Laboratory School in the Development of John Dewey's Philosophy of History," *The History Teacher*, Vol. 12, 3, May 1979, pp. 373-382.

7. Mary Hammett Lewis, *An Adventure with Children* (New York: Macmillan, 1928), p. 2.

8. *Ibid*, p. 4.

9. Leonard P. Ayres, *Open-Air Schools* (New York: Doubleday, Page & Company, 1911), pp. 3-5.

10. *Lewis*, p. 7.

11. *Ibid*, pp. 9-10.

12. Mary Finn, "Progressive Education in Amherst: The Park School," article for the *Colony Visitor*, republished by the Park School of Buffalo, 1978, pp. 25-26.

13. *Lewis*, p. 99.

14. *Ibid*, p. 96.

15. Dorothy Canfield Fisher, "A Peep Into the Educational Future," *Outlook*, September 1915, p. 215.

16. *Ibid*.

17. *Ibid*, p. 217.

18. *Lewis*, p. 21.

Note: A total of 23 photographs were included in the original text. Because of reproduction problems, these have been deleted from this reprint. New photographs from the archives of the Park School have been included in the Introduction.

x

AN ADVENTURE WITH CHILDREN

I

It must have had a beginning — adventures always do — but I have never been able to remember just how it started. This I know: When I was a young teacher, eager, afire with enthusiasm, it was my fortune to drop into a position in one of the best known and finest schools in this country. Here was everything that any reasonable teacher could wish, a spacious, pleasant room, with walls gently tinted to give the low-hung, admirably chosen pictures their precisely right setting. There was expensive school furniture, regulated to fit each child, as well as an ample library to supplement our classroom books. Best, and most unusual in those days of overcrowded rooms and un-

1

wieldy enrollment, there was a maximum group of not over thirty children. We had a curriculum most completely and carefully worked out and handed down to us from the highest sources of authority among the educators in the great university. We accepted it just as we did the paper and pencil supply.

But there had been growing upon me a firm conviction that something was radically wrong with schools everywhere. All my life I had played with children and found them inventive, imaginative, full of ideas, with never quite time enough to carry them out. Yet here in this school, a leader in schools in this country, we felt stifled, suffocated, when we tried to play, and as for teaching these children I know now that I never did anything which was more futile.

What the matter was I didn't know. Something was terribly lacking. In all this ready-made, standardized perfection, my own part seemed dishearteningly inadequate. When I tried to make people under-

stand my dissatisfaction with my own meager sharing in the education of these children, they unvaryingly replied with sincerest astonishment: "But what do you want? There is nothing anywhere better than this." And to that I had no answer.

I thought perhaps, if our room had a rug, a big, friendly rug on which we might sit together for closer companionship and comradely sharing of our interests, the feeling of unreality, of artificiality which observers with notebooks brought with them, might be dispelled. My principal, a man of remarkable tact and still more remarkable disposition, long tried by the vagaries of a nonconformist teacher, had never before been asked for a rug. A rubber plant or a Boston fern was a comprehensible request, but a rug was an eccentricity. However, tolerantly and resignedly he "O.K.'d" my requisition.

This did much to break up the formality caused by the rigid chairs and desks. To tell the truth, it became a sort of magic carpet in my adventure. The attitudes of the children changed completely the moment they set foot upon that rug. Language lessons became confidential chats about all sorts of experiences. One day the rug became early Manhattan Island; another day it was the boat of Hendrick Hudson. Unconsciously it began to dawn upon me that the thing I really wanted was to break up as far as possible the formality and artificiality of my classroom. But how was it to be done?

The next year, much to the relief of everybody concerned, our magic carpet settled the question. It carried us to the roof of one of our eight-story college buildings. There, in the windiest spot in New York City, under a huge canvas tent, we set up school-keeping. And it was there, after many months of living alone with the children, undisturbed by any grown-ups, untaught by any special teachers, in the most

primitive kind of environment, living day after day in the sunshine and doing all our own work, that it came to me. The thing above all else which these city children needed was a place to live in which would suggest ideas of what to do or what needed to be done, and freedom to carry them out.

We had bought a rabbit, and of course he needed a home. It was a dreary afternoon in November. We had no afternoon session, but as I was sitting under the tent I heard a boy whistling outside on the roof. I looked out, and there was a very small boy getting ready to shingle the roof of the rabbit house. He confessed that he had run away from home, that no one would know where he was; but "Oh," he begged in the most pleading tones, "please, please let me stay. If I go home, I'll just have to go to the movies." And I remembered that he was the boy who used to slip out and run home from school the year before.

Because we had very little furniture, we

made some of our own. The light on the roof was so bright that we made sunbonnets. In the spring we made a roof garden and raised radishes and lettuce. We prepared our own cocoa and served it, making quite a little ceremony of our luncheon, serving and chatting the while most socially about all the things that interested us. Instead of finding it difficult to break up the formality of the classroom, like Humpty Dumpty we should have found it almost impossible, now that it was smashed, "to put it together again." The outside observer, poor soul, studied us, if at all, as "an out-of-door school" and confined most of his questions to inquiries about "sitting-out bags" in cold weather or how well children could write with their gloves on.

Nobody ever guessed that there was born of this experiment a new conception of the education of little children and that the little New York City children learned something far more precious than the multiplication

tables, how to keep warm in an out-of-door school, or even to write well with their gloves on. They learned to love work because they could see its real significance. They had to be ingenious because the poverty of their equipment demanded it; the simplicity and naturalness of their surroundings made them their best children-selves; and they throve in that atmosphere of freedom and opportunity.

As for the teacher, well I knew that I never again should be able to go back to the classroom of even the finest school in the world. I was so thrilled by the discovery I had made that I had but one thought — to create a school which should be in reality a children's school — and nothing else in the world mattered.

With the joy of real discovery my courage was high. I realized, however, that under or even on the roof of this great building, with its expensive, luxurious, and, of necessity, artificial environment inevitable in a great city, was the last place in the world to try to establish such a school. Thousands of people went there to see good teaching, and they saw it. Nowhere else in the country could one see such skillful presentation of lessons. But somehow I had lost my interest in the presentation of lessons.

This year I had lived with children. I had heard them demand an all-day session because there was so much to do in the day's work. I had seen my most carefully planned lessons completely lost sight of in my effort to keep up with these busy people. I had learned more about the demands of little children during this year than I learned in all my years of study and experience. Such a thing as this happened: I had been struggling to teach an eight-year-old boy to read. He had thus far successfully resisted all attempts. I tried every method I had ever heard of and some which I hadn't. Finally, discouraged, I leaned back in my chair with a sigh. The boy looked up at

me sympathetically, and then with an effort to change the subject he asked, "Can you make an airplane?" I told him that I couldn't, and he replied cheerfully, "Oh well, I'll teach you." I told him that I was rather stupid in learning to do things with my hands and that he would find his task hard work. "Well," he replied generously, "no harder, I guess, than you find it to teach me to read." The relationship which grew up between children and teacher on this roof was of the kind I had never experienced before.

But this story promised to be an adventure, and it was at about this time, in the spring of 1911, that the adventure really began. A group of people from a middle-western city came up to our roof to visit. I was almost immediately struck with the fact that here were visitors of a different type from those I had been used to seeing. They were not in the least interested in the teacher and her plan of work. They were fascinated by the children and their activities. And no wonder. This was even before the article by Montessori had been published in one of our popular magazines and years before the words "progressive education" had been invented, and it was startling to them to come upon a group of happy children not on their own grounds at home but actually in a schoolroom, sanctioned by a great college, so utterly engrossed in their work that they didn't even notice the advent of a group of strangers.

Six or eight children were measuring the open part of the roof to see if they could afford the space to have another class up there next year and, if so, how much space would be left for a playground. A small boy was feeding a mother hen whose chicks were almost ready to hatch; a little girl had chosen a shady corner of the roof and was reading aloud to some of her mates who were making sunbonnets; a small boy was building the day's list of spelling words;

other children were making the morning cocoa. And these wise guests saw and understood.

Of course I told them my dream. The next day one of them came back and asked if I would go to ——, where their children lived, and let them help me start such a school. My great adventure had come!

I didn't know for years afterward what made the early years of the enterprise so stimulating and so successful. I found that Dr. Frank McMurry, who has been an understanding friend to many thousands of teachers in this country, had, on meeting one of the committee, begged her to let me work absolutely without interference for a period of three years, to give me everything within reason which I asked for during that time, and then to see whether the venture was worth backing in earnest. I leave you to imagine what that freedom and what appeared to be a remarkable faith on the part of the committee meant during the most critical years of this experiment, when parents and even some of our own teachers were skeptical of its value.

We started in a little rented cottage with no grounds at all. At the back of the cottage we built from each floor a rough porch. The downstairs porch we made into a kindergarten room. Above it, we housed on one side the first and second grades, and on the other, the third and fourth grades, with a partition between. Four courageous teachers, one of them a French teacher, composed the faculty. A very bright little girl of about fourteen acted as maid and secretary. These, with twenty-seven children ranging in age from three and a half to twelve, comprised our family.

For the first few days there seemed to be more mothers than children, and they were busy entering their children and taking them out again in a nervous sort of way. After all, this wasn't strange when you think that these children had been sur-

rounded by every luxury which money could buy, "hothouse plants" one of the mothers admitted, and we were proposing to keep them out of doors all winter in a most trying northern climate, in a crude environment which resembled nothing that the mothers had ever associated with a schoolroom.

After living through a few chaotic days, during which we as teachers were futilely attempting to convince parents of something of which we were none too sure ourselves, I suddenly thought, "Why, it was the children on the roof of the university building who convinced me," and with that I begged the mothers to leave their children with us without question for six weeks and told them that then we should meet and talk the plan over. I can never say enough for the splendid coöperation of those parents. Next to the children themselves it was they who started off the school. For it is one thing for a principal of a school to have ideas and be eager to try them on other people's children, but quite another thing for parents to take their children from established schools which they themselves have attended and voluntarily subject them to experiment.

The glowing eagerness which these youngsters carried home with them each day from school was absolutely irresistible. It isn't easy to remember the details of that first year, and anyway they were not significant. My own mind was filled with the school of my dream and always, consciously and unconsciously, I was looking for a place where it might become a reality. Certain things stand out in my mind, however, chief among which was the fact that once again here was the beginning of a children's school. A small place had been created in which children throve. I remember letters I received after visits from two distinguished professors of Columbia University (each of whom became during the succeeding year presidents of colleges), and each letter contained

this sentence, "I think they were the happiest children I have ever seen anywhere."

I remember, too, our effort to carry the simplicity and naturalness of the school living into out-of-school time. I found that the majority of these children were attending formal dancing classes, where, dressed in their best, including white kid gloves and patent leather shoes, and correspondingly miserable, they painfully learned the new steps in social dancing. And some of these tots were less than seven years old. I called together some of the mothers to see if I could find out why they were going to all this trouble and expense to have their children learn dancing steps which would become quite obsolete by the time the children were old enough to enjoy dancing. Most of them were sending their children because everybody else did; but there were a few who were quite sure that the children would acquire a certain grace which they could get in no other way, and one or two felt that courtesy might also be acquired.

I told them that I knew of a French Canadian who was a marvelous skater and who would, every afternoon during skating weather, take these children to the park lake, just a few minutes' walk from the school, and teach them to skate, and that I would almost guarantee the grace and even the courtesy. So, substituting for the white dresses and the white kid gloves and patent leather shoes warm sweater brownie suits and caps, these children, even the littlest ones, were soon swinging along across the ice with fearlessness and rhythm, singing as they skated, their faces glowing, their eyes snapping with excitement and pleasure. One look at them was sufficient, and the dancing school numbers were depleted.

The outstanding result of that first year's experience was but to confirm the conviction born on the windy roof of the college building. I felt sure that to create an environ-

ment in which children might live and grow and flourish, "a place in which a child's soul and mind might be at peace," was the all-important thing.

II

ABOUT this time some of the trustees, for such our committee had now become, began to consider plans for the following year. An architect had drawn up plans for a large, attractive brick building to be built around a court and almost to fill a three-cornered lot which was bounded on one side by a street-car track and on the other side by a cemetery. For this these enthusiastic people were going to raise $75,000. It makes me shudder even now to think how near we came to getting a three-cornered education in that very place.

But one of the men, seeing my discomfort and having many misgivings of his own, asked me to drive out to see an estate which he passed every day on his way home from the city. I shall never forget my first glimpse of that place, an old estate on the corner of the main street, an acre and a half

of land, grassed deep and shaded by some of the finest old elms I had ever seen, and in its midst an old colonial house, beautiful in its dignity. Although it had not been occupied for a long time, it looked as though it had been lived in by generations of children. It was springtime, and the birds were nesting close to the old house. The atmosphere of the whole place, with its possibilities as a home for our little school, was irresistible. This place would serve as a home for this family, with home-making processes in which even the smallest child might share. I took each trustee out there, with the final result that we decided to buy the property. I still have in my possession a letter from one of the men on the Board arguing strongly against it, stating that he was quite sure we should lose the thirty children we had and asking "what in the world we should do with all that land."

In the house we arranged for the family's meeting place, remodeling it to include a large, sunny living room with a great fireplace, a dining room large enough to hold over a hundred children, and a kitchen. The old woodshed became our shop. Keeping the colonial effect, we extended the porch to twice its size. Around the property, to insure a kind of privacy, we built a high green fence with a gate swinging in from the main street. The fact that we had no money to speak of was one of our greatest blessings. It resulted in our building around the main house five rough lumber bungalows open on two sides, and we became essentially an open-air school like the one on the roof of the high college building two years before, and for much the same reason. It seemed the easiest immediate escape from the artificialities of modern city living which are so disastrous to the wholesome, natural growth of little children.

We built houses for only as many grades as we had and planned to build a new house each year as we needed it. Our bungalows

were stained green and, by means of windows which dropped down into their casements, could be thrown entirely open on two sides in all fine weather. You may be surprised to know that all these rooms had formal desks and chairs. We had tried chairs and tables our first year and discarded them because with our out-of-door clothing we were always tipping them over and producing a cluttered effect in our schoolrooms. Anyway, we had come to the conclusion that it was not fixed desks and chairs but fixed children that we wished to avoid. However, our rooms were spacious, and in every one there was in some part of it a living-room effect, with rugs and tables and informal chairs, something of wicker with gay chintz, and I may say that most often the children were to be found there, working in groups or discussing or debating some question. It was our first-grade teacher who conceived the idea of individual cupboards built into the sides of the room.

She realized that the frequent jumpings up and down which were provided by this arrangement were very good for restless little people who were in school for the first time. There is scarcely a modern primary room to-day, sixteen years later, to be found anywhere which doesn't have children's individual cupboards.

These little houses took on the individuality and tastes of the families which used them and were altogether different, one from the other. One class even made a special little room by building a partition about six feet high with a small door, staining it like the rest of the bungalow. To this a child with a specially weighty problem might retire to work, a group might go to plan a play, or two children who had finished their work and who had trouble with adding might go to play dominoes.

As time went on vines were planted to run up over the houses. Little gardens were made, partly to add to the attractive-

ness of the setting, partly because children love to make gardens. Altogether, a sense of responsibility and pride grew up among the various groups as to the care of these little homes in which they spent so much of their time.

But the real sense of responsibility, as well as our greatest pride, was in our whole school. You see, fortunate as we were in not having money to spend, we were still more fortunate in having begun with a small family. We had, at the beginning of our second year, not less than thirty children, as was prophesied, but nearly a hundred boys and girls and a corresponding growth in our faculty. The nucleus of the first tiny school, a remarkable group of children, brought with them the wonderful spirit of the pioneer school, and it was no time at all before our family was at home in its new surroundings.

III

I HAVE been conscious all the time I've been writing of rushing along at breakneck pace to reach the real point of my story, where the dream school began, and now that I have actually arrived, I am overwhelmed with the difficulty of setting down on paper anything which will give you an idea of those thrilling early years of our life.

I think perhaps the only chance I have is by trying to show you that it was literally the children's school and that it was they who proved its great value. It was they who convinced the community; it was they, in their daily living, who made the school known all over the world. Dorothy Canfield seemed impressed in her one day's visit with that very thing. "They helped run that school," she said. "Their own conviction seemed to be that, if they did not,

everything would fall to pieces. And how they throve in that divine responsibility for the common welfare."

Amid these natural surroundings we developed our most natural selves, living much of the time in our own world of imagination and the rest of the time in utter absorption in our work and in the carrying on of our many duties. And this world in which we lived was as full of substantial meaning to children as the world of big business was to their fathers, and as replete with responsibilities. Our school became a joyous social community in which we lived. As we shared our interests and discoveries we formed good habits of community living and found out for ourselves that the joy of life comes from what we put into it.

The most beautiful part of our day's living was our assembly in the morning. A great open fire which had been laid and lighted by some of our early arrivals greeted us when we entered the room, and a veritable magician at the piano, who always seemed to know what music we wanted most, greeted us hospitably. We went in and sat down on the floor informally in groups, the smallest children in the middle. It took a long time for us all to be seated, but somehow the coming in, each with the silent, smiling greeting to everyone else, as though we were all returning home from a visit, was truly impressive, and in all the twelve years of our existence we never failed to look forward to it eagerly.

Some of the children called our meeting together "Chapel," and from that time on, although our exercises were sometimes anything but religious, Chapel it was always called. The chief thing which characterized our program was its spontaneity. Very often nobody knew what was going to happen. Sometimes the child who was leading would decide to have it entirely religious. We would repeat several of the most beautiful psalms, and we came to know many of

them from saying them over together. Even the youngest children learned them. One morning after Chapel, as I was taking a guest through the locker room we came upon a little boy of five, struggling to put on his wanagans (a sort of shoe which was worn for warmth over his other shoes) and having difficulty with knots. The thing which hypnotized us, however, and kept us standing there unseen by him was the fact that as he struggled he was repeating in the sweetest baby voice the words of the Twenty-third Psalm. And when his shoes were tied and he hadn't quite finished the psalm, he sat back with his hands clasped about his knees and went on, swinging in time to the rhythm, "Surely goodness and mercy shall follow me all the days of my life and I shall dwell in the house of the Lord forever." Then he trotted out to his classroom.

Usually, however, after repeating some of the psalms and the Lord's prayer and singing one or two songs, the little leader would say, "Well, what would you like best to do this morning?" And then came the natural, spontaneous sharing of experiences, a call for someone to tell all about the preparation for lunch, a question to the third grade as to what they were doing for the chickens these days and if they were still making money on them, a report from the fifth-grade children, who with their enthusiastic teacher had become real authorities on birds. Or someone would say, "I wish Kitty would play to us," or, "John, will you read the poem you made up about pirates?" Often the big boys would say, "Now, if you want us to, we will give you the rules for a game we want to play at recess to-day." Even a French play was sometimes demanded.

The noticeable thing was that, whether a child was asked to contribute or whether he voluntarily offered to do something, there was invariably an absolute lack of self-consciousness or sense of playing to a gallery.

This condition was not an accident. Just as truly as the perfect hostess knows how to produce an atmosphere in which her guests will thrive, so do those who understand children know how to surround them with an atmosphere which will bring out their truest selves. The hostess has her easy chairs drawn up about the wood fire, she urges the men to smoke, but it is really her own attitude of sympathetic understanding and interest in her guests which draws them out and makes them leave with the feeling that they want to come again. It isn't quite so easy with children. Anything which is in the least artificial or even very complex is naturally abhorrent to them, no matter where they have been brought up. An open fire, yes, but to sit on the rug is more enticing than to sit in any easy chair. Again it is in the attitude of the hostesses or teachers, it is in their genuine and not polite or feigned interest, in the real faith they have in children, that the secret actually lies.

Children are wonderfully true judges of their elders and of their relationships with them. Teachers, or any grown-ups for that matter, who have the real confidences of little children are very rare and privileged.

It is astonishing, however, how ingrained is our habit of assuming responsibility, even with all our faith in children. One year, on our last day of school before Christmas, we had prepared a simple service of some of the old carols, the Christmas story from the Bible, etc. Quite a number of distinguished guests were present. When our program was nearly finished, a little girl, evidently feeling that the program wasn't quite satisfying, rose to her feet and, without a trace of self-consciousness or forwardness, said, "Now, Miss ———, some of us have been getting up a little play, a Christmas play, and we can give it now if you would like to have us." I am ashamed to say that for the moment I experienced the same sensation that a mother or a teacher always has in the

presence of guests when children for whom they are responsible start to do or say something which hasn't first been approved by some older person. I turned anxiously to the child's teacher and found her looking decidedly worried. I was just ready to answer, "Some other time, dear," when I came to my senses and invited her very heartily to begin.

The play lasted ten minutes and was really a clever little play. Santa Claus in costume (it was because someone brought the costume that they invented the play) had found our large "Lost and Found Bag," which had been made by some of the older girls of the school to hold lost belongings. Because it helped to locate careless children, it was regarded by us all as rather a disagreeable thing. With this heavy bag over his shoulder, Santa came down our Chapel chimney into a room where two very poor little children lived. These children had been hastily clad in pajamas and a "nightie" borrowed from the janitor's child. When morning came, these children received with great glee the belongings of the careless school children, and the play was over; the moral was left to be inferred. We had succeeded in giving our guests a very good time, and the children in the audience were entranced. What we had done for the little children who had taken the responsibility of entertaining, it wouldn't be easy to estimate.

Many dramatic moments occurred during these impromptu meetings, but there was one which seems to stand out above all the rest. Again we were in Chapel at a time near Christmas, and again there were many mothers with us. The children had been singing like angels and had just finished their favorite carol, "Noel," when a baby child stood, a little girl only three and a half years old. Her tiny white skirts stood straight out about her, and she looked all around and asked the children, not me, "Would anybody like to have me tell a story?"

Her mother tried to grab her, but it was too late. The children eagerly assented, and slowly, with infinite pains, she told the story of "The First Christmas Tree." It was a long story, but she became so absorbed in telling it that she went on confidently. It seemed to me I had never heard the story more beautifully told, and as she stood there, swaying back and forth with no fear in her heart and a wonderful light in her eyes, she held us spellbound. I glanced from the big boys, who were devouring her every word, to the row of society women at the back of the room, and I found some of them silently weeping at the beauty of it all. When she came to the end, there was a deep silence in the room, and I had just presence of mind enough to signal to our musician to play for us to go out. We went quietly to our classrooms. It had been a breath-taking and never-to-be-forgotten event.

The baby went seriously back to her blocks in the kindergarten nursery, unconcerned and quite unaware of what she had done. One of the youngest teachers came to me, a great lump in her throat, and said, "Oh, how can we ever live up to this tremendous responsibility?"

IV

BUT of what did the more serious business of living on the part of these children consist? It depended upon the time of year and upon the things which needed to be done. I found the kindergartners one morning clearing up a neglected piece of ground near their house, carrying to a bonfire everything which could be burned and to another pile everything which could not, making the ground ready for sunflower seeds. When the plants came up, they weeded them and cared for them, and on the opening day of school in the fall gorgeous blossoms nodded their welcome to the new kindergartners. The seeds were fed to the third-grade chickens.

A group of the oldest boys spent all their spare time for three weeks making a concrete walk through our muddy orchard to the door of the shop. Almost any boy would be interested in a short cut to the shop; and as these boys had been watching the men mending the road, they were interested in making concrete. They needed a great deal of advice and help from the shop teacher; but the idea was theirs, their gang leader was of their own choice, and the coöperative labor of their own planning. Hence the great value of the undertaking.

One day as I walked into the fourth-grade house, I found them making up and solving problems in arithmetic about our janitor and his shoveling of the walks after a snowstorm. The first problem read, "If it takes one man so many minutes to shovel 836 feet of walk, how long would it take four men?" These children had tested "above grade" in arithmetic by all the tests which had been devised, and they were mentally very alert. The lesson was brought to a sudden halt, however, by a boy who said, "If the janitor had a snow plough, he could do it in no time at all." Another boy im-

mediately said, "Why couldn't we make the snow plough?" and still a third, "And we might run it." The teacher didn't seem at all disturbed by the practical turn which the lesson had taken and, turning to me, asked if they might have the lumber. The lumber was secured at once while the children wanted and saw the need for it and not at "some other time." When it arrived, the boys pounced upon it and, waving the driver aside, carried it to the shop themselves. Before the next heavy fall of snow, they were ready with a snow plough which met very satisfactorily the requirements of our walk. It would be hard to give you an idea of the delight of these boys as, with some first-grade children piled on for weight, they made their first trip around the 836 feet of walk. The fact that we looked to them on all snowy mornings after that for help gave them a sense of responsibility for service which was certainly a beginning in training for citizenship.

From my office, late one afternoon, I heard in the adjoining room this telephone conversation: "Oh yes, hello, Dad; you bet I'd like to go, but could you wait fifteen minutes? You see, I'm mending a broken window in the tower room. You know we are fixing up that room for our editorial staff. I've got the putty almost on."

I judged that "Dad" had agreed to wait. The companionship between this boy and his father was one of the finest things I ever knew. The family was one of our wealthiest society families, and I wished that the father could have followed the boy, as I did, through the old garret to the tower and seen him with his shirt sleeves rolled up and a pair of disreputable blue overalls on, his face grimy with dirt, putting in a new window pane very skillfully, in spite of the fact that he used a little more putty than was absolutely necessary. Since it was a self-imposed job, the boy, not the teacher, decided that he must rush up and finish it before he could join his father at the Country Club for a game of golf.

The longer I lived with those children, the more firmly I became convinced that we built wisely when we provided the simple, rough, stained bungalows for their school homes. There never was a time when some part of these little houses was not being reconstructed by the children. Bookcases were built in; tiny doors were cut to admit the family cat; a grocery store was made in one corner; trellises were put up for the newly planted vines; and window boxes were made, filled, and planted. Even ladders were constructed to enable the children to escape over the wall of the bungalow without the formality of going through the door.

Fortunately, highly skilled labor was not

20

required. All too often the results of children's carpentry work must measure up to an adult's standard of perfection or, what is even worse, to the standard of a manual-training teacher who holds his present job because accuracy in details means more to him than finding out what the world needs.

But here a ladder which would do the work was the main thing, and there was a good chance that the children in time, through this sort of purposeful work, would form standards of their own which were quite as difficult of attainment as those set by any teacher. It all depends upon whether children live in a place where there are plenty of things which a child can find to do and which need to be done and which he therefore finds great joy in doing. I have seen boys surmount obstacles under such circumstances which, if superimposed by some older person, would lead to the arrest of such person under the head of "cruelty to children."

The soft green stain of the walls of their houses made a lovely background for the sometimes startling color effects which children instinctively choose. In spite of our living in a very drab city with the minimum of sunshine, I have often heard visitors say, after a day or two in the school, that they remembered the city as full of color and sunshine and then realized that it was the remembrance of the happy children in their colorful setting which they carried away with them.

If a child marred the stain on the walls, he said nothing to anybody but rushed out to the woodshed, where there was an inexhaustible supply of green stain, brought it back, and did a little touching up. All this talk about green stain is to no purpose except that it helps to indicate how immeasurably environment counts in the education of children.

And so I shudder when I hear that a million dollars is going into a school building, and that not even a public school building in a large city, where there might be a little excuse for it. Prisons, they are, all of them, and deadening in their influence upon the precious qualities of childhood. I think they might be compared in their effect upon children to an apartment house with its killing "ready-made" effect upon family life.

Of course our lunch time was a time when service for the whole family was needed. The children organized, and there was each day a head waiter, often a child with real executive ability, sometimes a child who needed to acquire it, and an assistant, besides a waiter for each table. I don't yet know why it was always considered such a privilege to be chosen waiter. To be sure, these children ate by themselves after everyone else was through, sometimes had "two helpings" of dessert, and gave up part of their rest hour to clearing off all the tables, stacking up dishes, and brushing up the

dining room. And yet, the principal of the largest boys' school to which our boys went from our sixth grade said that, at the end of the first week of his school in the fall, he met two of our boys in the hall and stopped to tell them that they had received honors in their studies. At first they seemed to him unimpressed, but the next instant they asked eagerly, "Oh, does that mean that we can wait on tables?"

Once, a few years later, when the head of one of the most famous boys' schools in America visited us, he noticed a group of boys piling wood near their schoolhouse. He asked if he might go over and speak to them. Approaching the gang leader, he asked, "What time on your program are you using for this work?" The boy said, "Why, this is our playtime, sir." The head master came back to me with a puzzled look on his face and said, "Well, I could go back to my school and get my boys to pile wood; I think I could get them to make even a better woodpile than that, but will you tell me how you get your boys to *want* to pile wood?"

What was the secret of the joy these boys found in the arduous task of piling wood? Why did they "want to do it"? Undoubtedly the fact that they had never come to look upon the work as drudgery made a great difference. Everybody seemed to want to pile wood, and the spirit of the thing was very contagious. Of course, the magic way in which some of our teachers presented a job made a world of difference. But when all is said and done, I honestly believe that the "joy in the working" which was so bewildering to people on the outside, often to the children's own parents, came in this case chiefly from the fact that their own little schoolhouse needed the wood for its fireplace and its family looked to them to pile it. There was again the responsibility for the common welfare. You know what it does to you, after your theoretical belief in

some venture, suddenly to be put on a committee to carry it out. It changes your whole attitude, and you roll up your sleeves and pitch in. But here were children's attitudes toward work and habits of tackling hard tasks in the very making, and all that was needed was plenty of homely, useful tasks to go around.

I remember my feeling of alarm lest they shouldn't hold out; such opportunities seem to have so entirely disappeared from the modern home. But I needn't have worried. The teachers were as intoxicated as I was with this discovery and were continually on the lookout for tasks which had to be done, giving to the children the responsibility and the satisfaction of doing them.

The man who became president of our Board during the first year in our new home had more influence with the success of the school than he ever knew. He had formed the habit of coming to the school every morning during the summer, for he had agreed to act as a building committee of one, and nobody knows when our little houses would have been finished if he hadn't "jollied up" the workmen each morning and conversed over the phone behind closed doors with dilatory contractors and plumbers each day. Anyway, he so formed the habit of visiting these little buildings that after they were inhabited he kept on coming. I think that "jollied up" is a good expression for what he did for us all. He had only one little girl of his own, but he was adopted by innumerable children whenever he set foot on the grounds. The teachers used to look forward to his coming. In fact, we all seemed to feel that we could hardly wait to tell him what we had been doing and what we proposed to do next. Personally, I think our school would never have existed if it hadn't been for Mr. W——.

One of the many things he did for us one year was to make us want to adopt his hobby, that of raising bulbs. In so doing

he provided us with another opportunity such as we were searching for. As a result of his gift of bulbs, each and every one of us took part in a bulb-raising contest. There were in all a hundred fifty of us, children, servants, teachers, and principal, and each one had a pot of bulbs which after much study he cared for all winter. At about Easter time the bulbs, having been brought out of the darkness and tended most carefully, began to blossom. One morning we carried our pots to Chapel and set them on the floor beside us. Will you try to imagine how beautiful was this Easter garden of daffodils, narcissuses, hyacinths, gay tulips, and children planted on the sunny Chapel floor?

Once the problem came up of housing the janitor and his wife and little girl. There was a tiny apartment in the rear of the house which had not been finished off when we remodeled the school. The problem of painting woodwork, getting the room papered, and furnishing it was given to the oldest girls. They exulted in the idea, not only of deciding and choosing everything themselves, but of staining the furniture, making the curtains, buying the rugs and bed linen, and above all making a home for the new family. They had a limited time and very limited funds. They started off by choosing their favorite colors, when it suddenly occurred to them to ask the Polish wife what colors she liked, and their plans abruptly changed. A very fine relationship grew up between these girls and the Polish family, which resulted in the girls having much more consideration for them and the servants a greater tolerance for the children. The little apartment was both practically and artistically a success.

Building the chicken house for their very own chickens absorbed the attention of the third-grade boys and girls for a long time. It demanded judgment, ingenuity, and infinite patience. After the chickens were rained on one night it was the children who were worried, and not the teacher, for it was they who had shingled the roof. The discussion which I heard when the discovery was made was worth more than any cut-and-dried lesson I ever heard a manual-training teacher conduct.

V

ONE of the things I cared for most was to preserve the natural imagination of children and to let it develop to the greatest possible extent. Almost all children have it, but often it is crushed out of all recognition somewhere in the process of standardized schooling.

Never shall I forget the look on the faces of the children of the class who lived with me for a year on the roof of the high university building when they were given their first free play-period. They hadn't the remotest idea what to do with it. They simply stood and looked at each other, utterly helpless. Nor had they any better idea the next day, nor the next.

I determined not to aid them. I had none too much use for "supervised play"; and as to "organized" play, or "canned" play, as I have sometimes heard it called, of course everybody is organizing everything these days and children are easy to organize. But I wanted to discover if children had lost the art of imaginative play. I therefore remained inside the tent and waited. It did take a very long time, but one morning my patience was rewarded.

I heard a great shout from outside and rushed to the door of the tent, thinking someone must be hurt. Far from it! The shout was directed at me. I was being warned that my apartment was on fire. I must have been on the top floor, judging from the number of fire-escape stairs that had to be climbed by the firemen who were determined to rescue me. Below were the horses prancing and pulling at their bits (horses were still being used for the fire engines in New York). The crowd which had gathered was being handled by a brave policeman on horseback. A little to one side a newsboy was already calling out the news of the great fire. A long piece of pipe was being used as hose, and one boy's only part in the play was to make the noise of the water as it struck the house.

I was reassured from time to time by the heroic firemen as they fought their way up through the flames at my door. At last I was borne very carefully down all the fire-escape stairs — I am sure they didn't miss one — and laid on a grass plot. I thought the play was over and was about to assume my old rôle of school-teacher. Not at all. The baby was still left in the house! Again the heroic firemen rushed up the stairs. Of course the second time the feat was far more daring. They finally reached the top, found their way into the room, grabbed the baby (a large red pillow answered the purpose), and with a great shout tossed him out the window to the firemen below. The firemen brought him to me, and of course I hugged him and tried feebly to express my gratitude; but they had already jumped to the engine, and the bells clanged their way down the street. The play was over.

Something far more important than the mother and baby had been saved that day. Imagination wasn't lacking in those children. On the contrary, it was very vivid. It had simply lain dormant, that is all.

What I want you to feel with me is the importance of preserving at any cost such imagination as that. In these days of gymnasiums, organized plays and games, perfectly made mechanical toys, movies, and artificial standards of living, how can it be done?

Not always have I felt as much at ease as I did in this case. One day, as I went out into a garden where three children, the oldest seven, were playing, I was startled to have the five-year-old call out to me: "Say, would you mind climbing up into that tree and pretending you are God? We have a rabbit for it, but he keeps falling down."

The idea they had was to throw their dolls, together with tiny bits of white paper, up into the air. When the papers floated slowly to the ground, "Our babies have gone to Heaven; those are their souls," they breathed in a whisper. With true grown-up clumsiness I said, "But the dolls also fall to the ground." "Oh," they all said, with no tolerance for my stupidity, "we pertend not to see them." Of course I lost my chance of taking the chief rôle then and there. They infinitely preferred the rabbit.

I confessed my failure to the faculty after school, with the result that it was dark before we stopped discussing it. The conclusion we came to was this: In so far as it was humanly possible, we would not be guilty of blocking the way in the "pertend" stage of childhood so long as the school should live. We agreed that the natural imagination of children was the greatest asset we should ever have. Building on it instead of thwarting it would become an intrinsic part of our method of teaching. Since we were all playing the same game, self-consciousness, which is not a natural trait of children, disappeared.

If a group of boys in a class were pirates, they dressed as pirates, lived as pirates, behaved like pirates, and carried at their belts knives of their own whittling. When they came to the dining room for lunch, some of the smallest children scurried to tables at the other side of the room.

One day a Robinson Crusoe appeared. In the orchard I found some children living the lives of the Swiss Family Robinson on a rough platform which they had built in a tree.

Really great actors are great because they actually become the characters whom they represent in the drama. Children, if let alone, are truly great actors, and a thousand times better interpreters of Grimm's fairy tales, for instance, than almost any teacher who ever lived. They are impatient of descriptions or of too much detail in a story. They always look for dramatic action. They *live* in the story if not interrupted by too well-meaning adults. They forget everything and everybody. When they have finished, or perhaps the next day, you may stumble upon them somewhere and hear one of them say: "Let's play the story. You be the ——, and I'll be the ——." Then you will see true drama. If one of them feels that something exciting has been left out, he puts it in and his contemporaries seize upon it. Costumes are very hastily adapted and are effective; and as for scenery in the "let's pretend" stage of childhood, almost anything at hand can be made to do. Of course, the lines of the giant might be improved, but wouldn't you rather see a real giant and hear him roar than to hear the most carefully prepared lines of a teacher who hasn't been a giant for years? If only we could preserve this natural imagination of little children instead of talking about it, what a power it would be in this world!

We had an attic in our old building in which were many parts of costumes left there from time to time, and one of our greatest joys was to rummage about up there and find "just the thing," from fairy wings to seven-league boots. Everything was of the simplest, and the children filled in the rest. The plays were often crude, but it meant much to children to choose their own costumes and often to write their own plays.

In later years we had a marvelous art teacher who had been very successful in staging pageants in the city and who constructed for us gorgeous costumes, made often at a great sacrifice of her time and strength. This did a strange thing to our plays. We felt somehow as though we must live up to those costumes which had been so painstakingly investigated and made and which were always so very perfect. We hadn't hunted through books for them; somebody else had done that. They were provided for us "ready-made," having required no ingenuity on our part. Then they were produced (often by sitting up most of the night before) in time for the dress rehearsal. We hadn't lived in them. Our plays became rather finished productions; but the spontaneity and joy in the working had disappeared, and the real actors had vanished.

You might discover the actors again as you entered a class in American history and found yourself sitting in at a meeting of the First Continental Congress, hearing discussed with grave earnestness the problems of that period. Perhaps you would find the very children who had been quite satisfied with the crude lines which they made up as they went along in the early fairy stories three or four years later demanding dignified, imposing lines as they tried *Ivanhoe.* Alice in Wonderland lived as Alice for days. Roman and Greek history were vitalized in the minds of the boys and girls who lived through their thrilling pages. I often wondered if children who from the outset had formed the habit of putting themselves in the places of these famous people of history and fiction

wouldn't form the habit of understanding the other person's point of view in business and in politics, even to having a better understanding of international relationships.

Of course, living together as one great family brought about many lovely spontaneous happenings. One morning, as I entered our grounds after a light fall of snow I seemed for the first time to behold our spruce tree, towering over the roofs of the buildings. Suddenly I recalled the splendor of the first Community Christmas Tree of the year before in New York. Why not center all our Christmas festivities about our living tree out of doors? There was no one of our little buildings which did not look out upon the beautiful tree.

It is wonderful how the imagination of children, and of grown-ups too for that matter, works when the spirit is free. It wasn't more than two days after that before activities began, and everywhere they were centered about the tree. In all the little bungalows every sort of shiny and shimmery thing which could be devised by teacher or child was being constructed to hang from the branches of the great tree. In the shop, giant spider webs were made with silver tinsel to carry out the early legend of the Christmas spider webs. There were huge, shiny balls, and a wonderful star for the very top. In our English classes notes were written to children from far and near. The tree took on a personality of its own and wrote its prophesies of the night before Christmas. The arts fitted in; even the French teacher had all his classes make bright-colored fringed bonbons with a nut in each for the hungry squirrels. He was a genius teacher, our Frenchman. He had a beautiful voice, and sometimes you would hear it ring out across the grounds in a lovely French Noel. Even pop-corn strings were more interesting to make when you knew that the birds and squirrels were hungry and needed them.

"But didn't all this interfere with the work of the school?" you ask. Bless you, no! Our work was never so vitalized and meaningful, and work which is built around a Christmas tree which is to be shared with hundreds of children and many adults becomes so significant that its influence lasts. I remember one morning, when I came early to school, I was stopped by seeing on the front door a large sign which at first sight seemed to be a quarantine sign, but on further investigation I found that it was a demand from the third grade for more arithmetic. The sign read:

WANTED CHRISTMAS PROBLEMS
Eny kind will do.

The day before Christmas came at last, and with the help of two strong men with very high ladders and the children who came back to decorate, the electric lights and the many ornaments were put on and the tree was left in all its splendor.

The story of our first Christmas tree was so beautifully told by a sixth-grade child, who has recently graduated from Smith College, that even without her permission I shall use it, that you may see for yourselves the impression which such experiences make upon children. For that is the all-important thing.

THE CHRISTMAS TREE'S OWN STORY

I have always been proud of the fact that I can look over the tops of the other trees on our grounds, but I never was so happy about it as I was on Christmas Eve. Everything must have been decided very suddenly because not a whisper reached my ears until the day before Christmas when a great many children and some grown-ups came with the most beautiful, shimmery things that I ever saw. On my topmost branch they fastened a lovely star. All day there were many men on my branches, loading me with those lovely things. When the sun went down they left me in all my splendor.

At six o'clock the bells in the nearest church — those that ring on Sunday — began to peal. At this people began to pour into the gates, and the organ played. When there were about two thousand people in the yard it was quiet. I concluded afterward

that there really must have been fairies in the air, for suddenly I burst into a flood of light. I am sure my star on the topmost branch must have been seen for miles through the darkness.

Then those mortals sang all the Christmas carols the wind had taught me as I never heard them sung before. At first I thought it must be the Christmas angels. Then my lights went out and the people drifted silently away.

E. N.

If modern artificial environment and living tend to kill the natural imagination of childhood, how important a factor is the right kind of environment in the early education of children!

VI

DURING the first year of school, we felt, even in a place where we all agreed that children must be less restricted and where the work was purposeful and often necessary to the day's living, that unless we were careful, the work too often would be suggested, if not by the teacher, then by the need of the moment or the demand of the group. Where would there enter the element of choice?

Side by side with the capacity for service, education must give its children the means and the ability to use leisure time pleasurably. There must be "gentle pleasure and enjoyments that do not rush and roar, but distil as the dew." Certainly not from the grown people of to-day can children learn this. Increasingly, as time goes on, we are dependent upon being amused. We demand it. Being entertained with the least possible effort on our part is another indication of the times. I honestly believe that one reason why movies are so popular is that they make no demand whatever on intelligence. In the dark halls one doesn't even have to look intelligent. Movies undoubtedly have a great power for good and have done much to extend people's horizons, and they are going to do a great deal more. But don't you shudder when you hear a sixteen-year-old girl say, when you suggest *Les Miserables* for her to read, "Oh, I don't have to read *Les Miserables;* I have seen it in the movies"?

We concluded to set apart a time in the day's work in every class in the school when children should be encouraged to choose their own occupation. It is interesting to know that parents referred to this period as "playtime"; teachers called it "free time"; but to the children it was always "work time." Later in the high school it went by the name of "hobby hour."

This free-time period was in the last

analysis an opportunity for the expression of individuality. A child did precisely what his instinct led him to do as long as his chosen form of expression did not interfere with the rights of his neighbors. In these days when many of their elders are almost totally dependent upon artificial amusement, these children knew what to do with their leisure.

A boy might whittle a boat or saw the planks for a doll's house which his sister coveted; he might with infinite patience spell out upon the typewriter the day's list of spelling words. The room fairly hummed with activity. I have seen in a first grade of twenty children fifteen entirely different kinds of work going on at once. The boys whistled as they hammered; the girls sang or chatted as they made dolls' dresses. All were absorbed in their tasks.

To the teacher free time was a priceless opportunity for observation. She became the child psychologist. It was almost at once apparent which child was prone to

take the lead, needing to learn coöperation; which one was so timid that he must be encouraged to take initiative; which one too dependent and should learn to be alert and self-reliant. Through the deep understanding which came to the trained teacher during this time, no native tendency or talent was lost or wasted, but so guided that the child was started on the path toward intelligent and constructive living, with a resourcefulness which would make him adaptable to almost any conditions. Gradually we came to look upon this period as the most important one in the day's work. Guests, especially teachers, were apt to choose this time of day to visit the school. Gradually they became convinced that such a period of freedom would be possible even in large public school classes.

Three years after we experimented with this free-time period the primary supervisor of the local public schools told me that there was scarcely a primary school in the city whose program did not include such a period. This was welcome news indeed!

To-day there is hardly a modern primary school in the country which is not using this laboratory period. Other schools have carried it into the high school, as we did. Not long ago I heard of a university which incorporates a "hobby hour" in its day's program.

VII

I THINK that in many schools guests are looked upon as intruders. By the time we were five years old we averaged six visitors a day for nearly two years. The children were absorbed in their tasks and used to having people come in and out without ever interrupting their work. Our guests, far from being intruders, were stimulating and very often distinct contributors to the work of the school. Teachers and principals and superintendents from almost every large city in the country came to us. One morning we had an M. P. from England, two physicians from Austria, two Japanese students from Columbia University, the president of a great college, a superintendent of schools from the Middle West, and a Harvard professor, and what do you suppose I found all of us doing as hard as ever we could? Like all pedagogues we were swapping our theories about the education of children on the front porch while all about us were real children living some of these theories and killing others as fast as we were building them up. Of course, I scattered the guests as soon as I came to my senses and sent them about the school, but they returned to that central spot again and again to propound more theories, even though some of them had come a great many miles to see the children themselves. And we wonder why there is a gap of twenty-five years between the theory of education proposed by John Dewey over a quarter of a century ago and the so-called Modern School, which is just trying to put these ideas into practice. We talk too much, all of us, and observe and live with children far too little.

We had a very fine relationship with the public schools of our city through classes of teachers and principals at the university. We had teachers from the public schools almost constantly as visitors. At one time

one third of the public school principals of the city attended one of my classes at the university, and some of the finest inspiration and help we ever received as a school came from some of these public school people.

I remember once when about thirty principals came out to observe a lesson in world geography. After it was over and the children had gone, we went out to one of our school bungalows and "talked it all over" until nearly dark. Criticisms were freely given, and the teacher who had conducted the lesson was glad to get them. Bringing up public and private school problems for comparison cleared up many imaginary differences and made us each infinitely more tolerant and appreciative of the other's work. We went away with the feeling that after all, though the ways and means might differ, our real problem of meeting the needs of children was identical. It confirmed me in the opinion which I had often expressed, that the private school is justified in a democtacy only as it is enabled, through superior patronage, a better quality of teachers, less crowded conditions, and funds not provided by public taxes, to experiment along new lines of efficiency in education and serve as a fine type of research laboratory for the public schools of our country.

One day the thing which I had cared most to have happen during the first four years of the school suddenly came true. A telegram arrived from John Dewey saying that he would spend the following day with us. That great and simple man was to belong to us for a whole day. It seemed too good to be true. I decided not to tell any of the teachers who he was and to take him in as an everyday member of our family. Dr. Dewey had for so long been to us the great prophet and educational philosopher that I was a little afraid that the teachers, if they knew who he was, would not go about their usual work with the children without a certain degree of self-consciousness.

Dr. Dewey arrived as soon as did the earliest children, and from that moment he became quite literally a guest of the children themselves.

One little girl of five adopted him early in the morning and with her hand clasped tightly in his took him about the school, showing him all the things which she liked best. As they were about to enter the first-grade bungalow they met on the steps a little girl who was washing her doll's clothes in some delicious-looking soapsuds and hanging them on the lower branches of a near-by tree to dry. The five-year-old, greatly attracted, said to the baby-wash-woman, "I want to do that too," but the child was much too intent on her morning's work to pay any heed to the request. Finally Dr. Dewey, noting the persistence of his little hostess, interceded for her and said: "Won't you let this little girl help you wash your baby's clothes? Can't you find something for her to do?" With considerable reluctance the child stopped her work and, showing none too much toleration for the interruption, said: "If you want something to do, just go inside there and ask the teacher. *I'm* busy."

All day this man went about the school undirected. I found him now joining in an absorbing debate, later out on the baseball ground. After I left him during rest hour to rest in my office, I found on going back that he had left the office and was investigating a piece of land across the way to see if it couldn't be utilized for our next expansion. Another time I found him in the kitchen, a biscuit in each hand and a plate of biscuits on his knees, acting as a judge in the biscuit-making contest. He found the fourth-grade children planning a tour around the world — some of them lying flat upon the floor with their maps and atlases and all sorts of steamship and railroad posters, writing the advertisements for their special routes. Each child tried to get him

to agree to take his tour. At lunch time he sat at a table with some of the children, and I think I caught him quarreling with the boy who sat next to him as to which had the larger piece of candy. He was altogether the most delightful and the most understanding guest we ever had at the school. When four o'clock came and the teachers came up to my office to drink a cup of tea, they were greatly impressed to find that it was the noted philosopher who had been their sympathetic and altogether charming guest of the day and their joy was unbounded.

When one of them said to him, "Haven't you found visiting school for a whole day very fatiguing?" he laughed and said, "Why, you don't call this visiting school, do you?" We took that as a compliment.

He didn't leave until late that evening, and he doesn't know to this day what he did for that school in his one day's visit. I have been to him many times since, sometimes with great enthusiasm, sometimes with greater perplexities, but I have never left his office without renewed faith in the thing we were doing for children and a great inspiration to do more.

VIII

OVER and over again the question came to us, "But how do you manage your parents?" In the first place, there was never any thought of management. Making the school convincing and absolutely irresistible to parents was one of our chief jobs; and of course while we depended largely upon the demonstration of our ideals, there were constant questions and misunderstandings.

Two things were absolutely necessary. First, we must show parents that we were doing our own thinking as a school, and that we had a definite educational policy, a policy which was the result of an endless amount of thought and planning of teachers who were giving the best part of their lives to bring it about. This policy we should adhere to if we lost every child in the school. Patrons' letters never began, "If you as a group of parents will agree, etc., we shall be glad to try, etc." or "If enough parents desire, etc." Invariably we said, "We have decided to adopt the following plan."

Second, there was never a time when our teachers would not give up hours of time, if needed, to explain plans and methods. It was impossible to conceive of building up a radical venture of this sort without the help and coöperation of fathers and mothers.

"How do you prevent parents from meddling in the work of the school?" was another constant question of educators. This was accomplished in several ways, one of which was to make them feel that they were always welcome as visitors to the school. Mothers brought their knitting and stayed all day. At lunch time they were the guests of their own children, and a mother who had asked me in my office the day before what I should do if children threw oatmeal across the table, as hers had done at breakfast, must have had a mixture of feelings as she sat down with her boy at a table with four-

teen children and no other adult. Not only did she see him eat just what was put before him as a matter of course, but she found that he was the life of the little company, while her little girl of ten was acting as head waiter with the remarkable efficiency which she inherited from her mother. Children who feel responsibility for the success of something which belongs to them would not think of doing a thing that would deliberately defeat that end.

Except as visiting parents were brought in to serve as a motive, as, for example, to hear an interesting story or to act as judge in a relay race in arithmetic, they went quite unnoticed by the chief actors in the scene. Work was altogether too absorbing, and the seriousness with which the children went about their tasks made it impossible to think of interrupting them. A father of a boy "who is as restless as the day is long, who has no power of concentration whatever, and who won't stick to anything five minutes" watched him silently from the back of the classroom for forty minutes and then slipped out unnoticed, saying, "Never would I have believed it if I hadn't seen it with my own eyes." No one was making that boy work with such intentness and concentration; nobody had attempted to "make the work interesting." The *work itself* was interesting and demanded every ounce of attention which the boy had. It was he who cared most for the achievement of this hard piece of work, not the teacher.

Questions we asked parents were of this order: Is your child fatigued after his day's work? Is he becoming an investigator? What interests does he bring home? Does he show more initiative than he used to? Does he eat and sleep well? Is he eager to go to school? Parents came to know that we depended upon them enormously for help, and they gave it freely. They came to understand too that on the other hand we should no more expect them to criticize a

teacher for a method she was using in teaching the multiplication tables than they would expect one of us while lunching at their house to ask them why they gave their child white bread instead of graham.

We never entirely persuaded parents that criticisms of the school brought straight to the principal's office could be used constructively in the growth of the school. It was much easier and a little more interesting to pick up the telephone and say, "Have you heard that out at the school, etc.?" Criticisms of this sort resulted in their gathering momentum like any other gossip and assuming an importance out of all proportion to their relative value and served as a detriment to the progress of the school which we all had so much at heart.

Some days I was in despair, and it seemed as though we hadn't gained an inch. I remember going up to my office utterly discouraged one morning. When I opened my office door, I came into a room which at first glance might have been covered with a light fall of snow. My Airedale puppy, restless under confinement, had chewed up several down pillows. There he sat on the couch in the midst of great drifts of down, only his nose and eyes visible, vainly struggling with his paws to brush away the down and work his way through. It was a funny sight to see him so completely baffled and making absolutely no impression upon the clinging down. But I knew exactly how he felt. We had to use the vacuum cleaner on him and upon the rest of the room. It occurred to me suddenly that perhaps a vacuum cleaner was the thing we really needed to use on education.

However, when you realize that this was one of the first departures in this country from the conventional type of school and that not only had these parents no experience of their own to rely upon but none anywhere else to refer to, you will agree with me that they showed considerable faith in

the undertaking when they allowed their children to continue in the school. I shall always believe that I came upon an unusually intelligent group of parents in that midwestern city and that but for their courage and intelligence and sustained faith the little school would never have grown up.

Among our many parents' meetings, all of which were remarkably attended, the most successful one was the one to which I invited only the fathers. They came because I wrote them that I didn't think much of the way in which the responsibility of deciding about the education of children was being handed over to women and asked them if they were making any more important investments anywhere than in the education of their own children.

The fathers all came. The mothers came along because they wanted to find out why I had called a fathers' meeting. We stayed until late that night. The questions up for discussion were vital ones. What are the qualities demanded for good citizenship? How responsible is the school as a factor in developing these qualities? The strongest points that were brought out were these:. that children should be led almost from the beginning to think independently, to make decisions of right and wrong and to act upon them courageously, to regard the rights of others with whom they worked and played, and to work coöperatively for the best good of their community. We discussed too the enormous importance of assuming responsibilities and brought out the fact that children who were constantly being given a chance to take responsibility were getting from day to day the finest kind of training for the recognition of and attack upon civic responsibilities which would come to them when they were men and women.

I don't want you to think that we stayed constantly on that high plane. It was a father and not a mother who stood just at this point and said in a slow, nasal drawl,

"Yes, but I want to know what to do when my child comes home with only one overshoe."

However, we all left the meeting that night with a renewed feeling of the great responsibility which devolves upon us as parents and teachers in this task of educating future citizens. No man who attended the meeting that night was ever too indifferent or too busy to make the trip out to the school whenever an opportunity was offered.

At other times we discussed more specific problems. A letter like the following went out:

There will be a demonstration lesson in arithmetic in the fourth-grade class Tuesday, May 24, at nine o'clock, to which you are cordially invited. A discussion of the lesson will follow in the assembly room. Again it is requested that no mention be made of this lesson to the children so that the work may be as free and spontaneous as possible.

The discussion after the lesson, with the teacher present, gave a chance for all sorts of questions and a clearing up of many misconceptions. I remember a father who had a little girl without a strong mathematical sense saying that he had great difficulty in helping his child at home because "methods nowadays are so different." In division the child insisted that the answer must be put above the line instead of below. The father looked greatly relieved when I told him that, as far as I was concerned, she might put the answer out on the back porch if it was the correct one.

The fact that there was "method in our madness," a real science back of our methods, and that our fundamental aim was coincident with theirs — namely, to give the children a real conception of numbers and speed and accuracy in the manipulation of figures — was apparently a new idea to many of them. They could see, too, that mathematics, like everything else, is more easily grasped by children who can see the uses to which it can be put, that there is, therefore, absolutely no excuse for the sort of mental

paralysis which seems to attack a child of a fifth grade who is confronted with a problem in fractions and who will say to you, "Well, if you will tell me whether to add or subtract or multiply or divide, I can do it."

But as the scope of the school increased and the clientele doubled in numbers, it became more difficult to keep this close touch with parents. The number of guests increased amazingly. We began to discover that the school was actually better known to people abroad than to the people of our own city. A woman who came all the way from Colorado to visit the school spent the night with a woman in the city who had never heard of it. A woman principal from England, sitting in my office one morning, showed by her intelligent questions about some of the experiments we had been trying that she was in very much closer touch with our work than were some of our own public school principals.

I therefore sent out the following letter, with a copy to the newspapers:

To our patrons:

The —— School will be open to all patrons of the school on Washington's Birthday. During the day there will be observed a regular "day's work," the object being to acquaint as large a number of people as possible, parents and educators, with the *actual work* of the school. We are choosing this day in order that business men may feel that they can spare the time really to investigate the work which their children are doing.

On this day there will be the program of the "day's work" in compact form, like a time-table, which will show every guest exactly what is going on with every child and every teacher every minute of the day. There will also be large signs printed by the children showing location of buildings, etc. In this way it may be possible for a guest to follow up a subject like English straight through the day, or a grade, or an individual child through his day's work. By following starred subjects, it will be possible for a person studying curriculum to visit almost every kind of work and social activity during the day. The business of educating the children of this generation is a mighty serious one, and you can't afford to leave it entirely to us.

Lunch will be served to guests in the main building at twelve thirty o'clock.

Come and bring others with you!

Faithfully yours,

Hundreds of people came, among them, over two hundred teachers and principals. Some of them stayed all day. No change was made in the work of the school, the only change being in the organization of the program to enable people to see typical work all over the school. And because there was no attempt to play to the galleries, the children soon caught the spirit of the thing and its sincerity of purpose and worked with few exceptions as naturally and normally as usual.

I wonder if it was because of my experience of nearly a quarter of a century with little children which brought the confidences of many young mothers to my little office. I don't believe any doctor or minister who ever lived has received more. Of course, I have always claimed one superior advantage over mothers. Their children were ten years old but for a year, and before they were able to decide what was the very best thing to do for a ten-year-old he was eleven. By the time they had given much time and thought to problems of adolescence their girl was ready for college, while my children stayed the same age for a long time together. I had worked and played with ten-year-old children for twenty years.

I was asked occasionally if these conferences with mothers bored me. On the contrary, some of the most worth-while and most cherished hours of my life were spent with mothers in my office, and any success which I may have had with children is due far more to those quiet conferences than any one will ever know.

Once, I remember, it became necessary to send for both father and mother of a boy in the school to tell them some pretty appalling facts about their son. He had been associating with a gang of foreign boys near his

street and had picked up some shocking language and ideas. It was necessary for me to produce some proofs in order to get the parents to believe me at all. It was a very heart-breaking occasion. The father asked in desperation what he should do. My answer, as nearly as I can remember it, was this: "The boy doesn't see enough of his own father. Can you possibly drop everything and take him up into Canada camping with you for three weeks?" He did it. They each came back to business the better for it; but, further than that, there grew up a relationship between the father and the boy which meant the salvation of the boy and untold satisfaction to the father. Try to imagine what might have happened if the school had followed the line of least resistance and expelled the boy.

Not having anything very tangible and definite to use as a standard by which to measure the school's efficiency, parents would sometimes say, "Yes, but I want to know how my child compares with a child in the——— School (naming one of our rival schools)" or "My child is having Europe in seventh grade while so and so at the ——— School is studying Asia." (Asia came after Europe in the geography textbook.) I answered that, if I found one of our teachers taking up the study of Asia during these years of the World War, I would discharge her. Of course, I had to explain that children who were studying Europe when all the world was studying Europe and geography was being made over would have a knowledge of Europe that children who had studied it before or after could never hope to have.

At about this time an Englishman who had a very bright boy in the sixth grade came into my office one morning to withdraw his boy from the school. I expressed some dismay, and he said: "I asked David last night to tell me the population of Liverpool and he failed. He couldn't even describe accurately the course of the Thames River.

And he tells me he is studying England!" I remembered the glowing face of this boy as I had heard him the day before discussing with his classmates the contribution which England and her colonies were making industrially to the work of the War and I asked, "But what did he answer to these questions?" "Oh," said his father in utter disgust, "he said, 'I don't know, Dad, but just give me a second and I can look it up for you.' "

"Do you know, Mr. G———," I said, "that if you had worked for months, you couldn't have paid the school a greater compliment. The fact that your boy isn't cluttering up his mind with statistics when he needs to use it for thinking shows a discrimination which many men do not possess. Of course you realize that at this time the population of Liverpool doesn't stay the same for two consecutive days." The boy remained in the school, and the father eventually became one of our most loyal patrons.

However, there were two real fears expressed by parents too often to be ignored. One was the fear that their children weren't getting the moral and disciplinary value correlated with hard work and the other, that they were not "covering the ground" in the three R's. These fears arose solely because the children were happy. Parents remembered well the grind of their own school days. Being miserable was so closely associated with their work that they looked upon it as a necessary accompaniment. We gave our children the standard tests, and they tested in the three R's above grade. But that made very little impression, even though these tests had been tried upon thousands of children in this country in similar grades. I called attention to the fact that the only men and women in the city who were making any real contribution to civic welfare were men and women who were in love with their jobs, that there was no escape from drill and drudgery, but that, where there is motive for

work and joy in achievement, drill and drudgery are tackled, if not happily, at least hopefully, and that the great desire for achievement enables one to surmount any obstacle. I persuaded them to read John Dewey's book on *Interest and Effort in Education,* for nothing written on the subject has ever been more convincing. At last the idea occurred to me that I could give them exactly what they wanted. Enough of our boys had left the school at the end of the sixth grade for other schools, run by standards which these parents understood, to formulate some statistics. Our girls were still with us. I therefore sent out the following letter with the statistical enclosure.

To our patrons:

To-day we realize as perhaps we never have before that we *must be able to judge intelligently the work of our schools.* If a democracy demands citizens who shall be serviceable, efficient, coöperative members of a community; if it demands that these citizens shall be able to think clearly and independently, have the courage of their convictions, be able to assume responsibility, and have a respect for the rights and opinions of others; if it expects them to attend with honest effort and promptness to life's obligations, we must measure our schools by their ability to develop such qualities in the years in which habits are formed.

It is going to take a long time to readjust our standard of measurement of the efficiency of a school to these requirements. For a century, our one test of schoolroom efficiency has been the ability of children to pass examinations to enter the next grade or some upper school. What possible chance has there ever been to gauge from the results of these written tests the development of any one of the qualities which we are demanding from our full-fledged citizens?

When I hear from as many as ten principals of upper schools in different parts of the country that our boys and girls have a fine attitude toward work, that they think and reason well, that they have formed good habits of work and study with economy of time, and that a large proportion of them have reached the upper schools with qualities of resourcefulness and initiative which make for leadership, I believe that, in spite of our many mistakes, we are on the right track, and I am glad that it has been in these respects a single track for the nine years of our existence.

However, a school which has for so many years been consistently working along these lines ought also to measure up to the old standards with no difficulty whatever. Its pupils should be able to do the

academic work of other schools with ease and with credit.

I have made a careful investigation of the standing of every boy who has left the —— School after at least three years' work with us, both because I thought it might be of interest to patrons and because I was really curious to know just what happens to our children when they enter other schools. I chose to make our first record of boys rather than girls because, since our boys leave the school at the end of the sixth grade instead of the eighth, we have a larger number of records from which to judge.

I submit this chronicle to you without further comment.

Faithfully yours,

SUMMARY

OF

BOYS' REPORT

Total number who left the school after three or more years' attendance 37
Number of different schools represented . . . 15
Number who "skipped" a grade on leaving or since leaving —— School 19
Number who have been retarded on entering any other school 0
Number who are termed "honor" students . . 15

Number of whom principal of school says, "Fine
work" 2
Number of whom principal of school says, "Very
good work" 5
Number of whom principal of school says, "Good
work" 4
Number of whom principal of school says, "Fair
work" 9
Number of whom principal of school says, "Un-
satisfactory work" 2

These were tangible results. Here was
something to hold on to even when assailed
by parents of rival schools, whose doubts
vigorously stated had been tending to under-
mine our parents' none too stable convictions. This report was a great time saver
as well. As soon as we heard the inevitable
question, "But what about these children
when they must go to other, more formal
schools, with a high standard of scholarship?"
one of these reports was much more satisfying than any argument.

This phase lasted a comparatively short
time when there was started a new question,

"Will the children of this school be able to
pass college entrance examinations?" It
would be some years before we could answer
that, and yet some of our children had already sent applications for entrance to our
large eastern colleges. Rival schools of the
city were able to point with pride to long
lists of students who had passed college entrance examinations with honors. In vain I
argued that boys and girls who had acquired
a fine attitude toward work, who had developed an "insatiable intellectual curiosity,"
who had been, without exception, able to
meet successfully the conditions of other
formal schools would not only be able to pass
the entrance examinations but would carry
with them into college the spirit which had
characterized their earlier work and would
therefore profit far more from college than
we had. In vain did I point to the fact that
the prophesy was coming true which I had
made at one of our earliest parents' meetings,
in 1912, that a great change would come

about in entrance examinations, that they were breaking down before our very eyes, and that there were being substituted tests of general intelligence, tests measuring the abilities of students to get the most out of college work, and the judgments of teachers and principals. The fact remained that it was a very serious question.

I had seen some of the criminal results in schools where the end and aim, the goal toward which they were working at any cost, was to enable pupils to pass the college entrance examinations. Were we to lose sight of the ideals toward which we had been consistently working all these years? Were our teachers to change entirely the standards toward which they had been working? I should rather have had smallpox infect the school. I can imagine nothing which would have been more utterly destructive. The only thing I could do was to call parents together and tell them frankly what our stand would be. Frequent teachers' meetings, es-

pecially among high school teachers, were also called to discuss the question. My answer was invariably this: "We shall not in a single instance sacrifice our ideals. If, when our girls and boys reach their senior year, it is necessary for them to have several months of intensive work in preparing for examination, it will be given to them." Several anxious parents withdrew children who had been with us for years, to give them two years in a school which *guaranteed* passing college entrance examinations; but we held to our beliefs.

One of the most illuminating articles which I have run across on the subject of "college entrance" was written by F. S. Broun for the *Atlantic Monthly*, January, 1925, under the title "Preparing for College in Eleven Months." In this article he tells how he, a country boy on a Michigan farm, at the age of fifteen prepared himself to pass creditably college entrance examinations in eleven months, with no aid from teachers. If this was possible, why in the world should we greatly restrict our curriculum, sacrifice our ideals, seriously impair the habit- and attitude-forming years of childhood and adolescence by introducing so early the college entrance goal?

To quote from Morgan Barnes, who wrote for the *Atlantic Monthly* on the subject "Procrustes Redivivus. The Cause and Effect of College Examinations": "A nationally known writer on educational subjects, a teacher whose interest in educational process is keen and constant, recently declared to me that he would rather have his own boy forego the advantages of college life than have him subjected to the blighting influence of deliberate and exclusive preparation for the present system of entrance examinations. . . .

"Faith in figures as measures of the undimensioned is slow to be renounced, and the fiction of the examination's vital and final significance is inveterate. But may there

not be educational as well as theological One-Hoss Shays?"

Since then several of the best schools in this country have taken the same stand about college entrance examinations, notably the Lincoln School in New York. If college demands continue to be tests which do not coincide at all with the ideals we have for education and still we wish to be sure that our children will enter college, what else is there to do except to set aside two or three months at the end of the high school period and sanction cramming? If a country boy with no help could do it, certainly, with the foundation which we had given, with the habits our children had acquired of being able to concentrate on and achieve hard tasks, and with teachers to help, we could do it and do it creditably.

One Monday morning in the spring, when our babies who had started with us in kindergarten and first grade were finishing their tenth year of school, I asked fourteen of them who had been entered for Smith to come into my office to help me decide something. I had overheard some of their conversation about college and realized from it that their notion of college was very vague and had been noticeably colored by the inevitable discussions which they had heard about the bugbear of entrance examinations. The question of "getting into college" was the main thing. Nobody had gone on and wondered what it was like to live there.

The question I put up for discussion was this: "How would you like to run away from school Wednesday night this week and go down to visit Smith College for four or five days?" I explained to them that one of their teachers had agreed to chaperon them and would be able to get rooms for them in the Graduate House. If I had proposed visiting the planet Mars, they wouldn't have been more bewildered. Visit a real college? Had such a thing ever been heard of before?

I told them that in the hope that they would like my plan I had made their reservations for them on the train both ways, told them just what the cost would be, and said that all that remained for them to do was to persuade their parents to let them go.

Unless you can look back to the time when you were a thirteen- or fourteen-year-old girl and were met by such a proposal, you can have no idea of the excitement which prevailed. It was quite typical of the girls' powers of persuasion and of the fine coöperation of the parents that every girl went. I didn't receive so much as a telephone inquiry about it from a single parent.

I had written several of the professors that the girls were coming, and I can never say enough for the fine cordiality with which they were received. They were given front seats at the intercollegiate basket-ball game; they attended Chapel and were profoundly impressed with the dignified formality of the services and the words of the president; they attended freshman English classes and freshman Latin classes; the professor of music played the organ for them; they were invited for tea to the rooms of one of the English professors. Altogether, I venture to say that nothing which they had ever done or ever would do would be much more thrilling to them than were those days of living on the campus of one of our large colleges at the time in their lives when impressions were very vivid and very lasting. They idealized college, of course, but why not? Wasn't that in itself something of a preparation for college?

They came back to breakfast with me after a never-to-be forgotten experience of the kind which has more influence than can easily be gauged, and with them I lived through those marvelous days when they were allowed to stand on the edge of Smith College and look in.

Not only was there no loss in their own school work, but there was of course a new

meaning and inspiration which influenced all their work, and there was what was far more important, the right kind of outlook into the immediate future.

After the school had been running along for eleven years and our parents seemed in danger of again sinking back into the attitude of accepting the school without quite enough question, I wrote them a letter. I told them that I thought we, parents and teachers, were apt to lose sight of the goal toward which we were really working in educating our children, that we were prone to focus on the thing too near at hand. I asked them to let me know what equipment they thought their own boy or girl should have, say at the age of eighteen, to meet the adventure of life. And I asked them what combination of studies, environment, companionship, and experiences they thought would be most effective in making this equipment.

The result was most interesting. Parents

for the most part were absolutely nonplused. Were they not paying tuition to have their children educated? Why should they be asked to do any thinking? One man wanted to withdraw his children at once.

But one morning, when I received the following letter from one of our mothers, I felt sure that we had not been working in vain, and that our great secondary aim was a little nearer achievement — namely, to educate parents to demand intelligently the right sort of education for their children. How many parents do you know who, if asked such a question as the above, would write such an answer?

My dear Miss ——:

Your letters have set me dreaming, and in my dream I see my girl at eighteen, erect, clear-eyed, full of joy of living, a thinker, eager in her search for truth, a believer in goodness, an unconscious champion of justice and brotherhood.

I believe that education should be directed to these ends, that the mind should be trained to work in

straight lines, that the perceptions should be cultivated, that teachers should be chosen for spiritual qualities that will make them a perpetual inspiration to their children.

As to a specific course of study — how can that be made? I doubt not that often the sprouting wings of genius have been ground down in the mill of college preparation work. If mathematics does not teach my daughter to reason, should not some other way be found to help develop that all-important faculty? What will do it? A student of psychology or pedagogy might give the answer, but I can't.

For myself, I count no blessings greater than a love of nature (and in nature one need not necessarily exclude one's fellow men!), for to me it implies sound faith in God's goodness and makes impossible slavery to artificial standards. Freedom to express oneself in language or in music or in some other form of art I should put next in the order of factors making for happiness.

Whether the reading of great books is more helpful in cultivating a vocabulary than the study of Latin or Greek would seem to me again to be an open question. I should think that it would have to be settled by a consideration of individual cases.

Surely the "spark" is in most young minds. It is only a question of kindling it. I believe you are doing just this — and you are blazing a trail that will lead to we know not what glorious vistas. Good luck to you and courage!

You see I'm a muddle of "feelings;" very unhappy sometimes that *my* education didn't help *me* to straighten them out and perhaps even harness them to useful ends.

I'm afraid this is not a bit what you wanted, but I'm glad you asked the question, for my dream has been a happy one!

Sincerely,
A mother

From our men came a great variety of answers. A large percentage of them didn't get beyond the question of passing the college entrance examinations. And yet what standard of measurement did they have to guide them further than their own personal experience? Many of them were thoroughly dissatisfied with their own education, but after plunging into business they had done very little thinking about what had made it inadequate.

This letter came from a father of four boys, a man who did a great deal of independent thinking:

Dear Miss ——:

Some years ago I could have answered your letter of May first with assurance, but now I hesitate to offer any suggestions. I have seen the woe wrought by so many well-intentioned, well-laid plans that the more I see of the past, the less sure I am of the future. When I was graduated from college, I knew that what a boy needed was more science, a better vocabulary, a knowledge of the woods and fields, and a reasonable amount of mathematics; but since then I have met men whose lives have been made happy by their great knowledge of the use of the subjunctive mood in Latin, and if I were the father of a boy who might become such a man, I should regret that I had deprived him of reveling in the subjunctive mood to make him drudge through life as a chemist or banker.

Not having yet been able even to guess at the future of my boys, I dare not try to shape their future thoughts.

One thing is almost certain. They will be American citizens. Therefore, they must be taught the privileges and also the duties of that citizenship.

They should know about the history of their country and the theory of its government, and this requires a knowledge of the history of other nations. They should learn to respect the rights of others, and from my observation you seem to have instilled this into them. All that I can say is: give them science, a better vocabulary, a knowledge of nature, all the mathematics they will absorb (mine will not get soggy) and later give them some Latin; and if they show a predilection for the uses of the subjunctive mood, give them lots of Latin, even at the expense of what I should consider more useful knowledge.

Sincerely yours,
A father

And then came a letter from one of our own teachers. I saw no reason for exempting the faculty from this experience. This letter was written by a teacher who had never had a child of her own and probably never will have. For the sake of education, I hope she may continue as a teacher as long as she lives.

My dear Miss ——:

When "my boy" is eighteen, I wish him to have insatiable intellectual curiosity, a fine sense of spiritual values, a well-developed, strong body, a generous tolerance, a faith in his own power to achieve, a happy comradeship with boys and girls, men and women, and a zest and joy in mere living.

I expect the school to help rather than hinder in the

achievement of these ends. It must not fit this boy into its scheme, but adapt its scheme to him. I expect the school to recognize him as an individual rather than treat him as the "typical child." It should encourage and direct his special aptitudes and abilities as well as develop and train less apparent but essential powers.

Believing with Henry Adams that "he knows enough who knows how to learn," I expect the school to help furnish the intellectual tools and to stimulate rather than deaden his desire to use them. I do not particularly care what form the curriculum may take or when or where it may prescribe certain studies. I do care exceedingly that whatever he does shall have meaning for him, that the content be rich and varied, including modern languages from an early age, ancient languages to the degree that he shows ability for them, and a great deal of science from experiences of outdoor observation and discovery and from indoor, laboratory experimentation, and that he be so stimulated in all his undertakings that his intellectual reach shall ever "exceed his grasp." I expect, of course, that history and geography shall not only have present significance, but shall form a basis for intelligent, sympathetic understanding of economic and social conditions as he will find them.

I ask that his poetic imagination be fostered and directed through exposure to that art, that music and literature be selected from the old and the new which interprets and enriches life for him in terms of truth and beauty. I ask that he be urged to express himself creatively in whichever medium he may show ability. If he has the inquiring mind which seeks satisfaction through measuring itself with more mature, more trained minds, both among people and in books, he will not lack the language to express his ideas.

I expect the school to help supply him with a democratic companionship of boys and girls with whom he competes in work, free play, and organized sports. I expect the school to place definite obligations upon him for which he is held responsible. I expect it to supply him with teachers of culture and character, with a deep and true understanding of children rather than a theory of education.

If his home coöperates and supplements his school through giving him every possible, wholesome, liberating experience — travel, opportunity for exploration and discovery on land and water, animals to care for, good books, invigorating friends, sympathetic, comradely relations with his parents — then surely the goal which I have set for him may not be unattainable.

A teacher

On the whole, these letters did much to shake us all up and bring us together again, with the aim of our work set forth anew.

IX

THERE was in this school from beginning to end no awarding of rewards and no inflicting of punishments as these are usually understood. It would have seemed as utterly incongruous to these children to have had these artificial stimuli as to have seen their fathers come home from their offices bedecked with red or blue ribbons to indicate how well they had put in their time during the day.

I well remember when a new teacher came to us from a large public school system to take charge of our shop. She was popular almost from the start, both because of her own personality and because of our admiration for the remarkable dexterity with which she used tools. Some of the children were a little surprised when on dismissal from the shop they were made to stand in a line and, as they went out, presented with lovely gold letter *E*'s.

I watched this with some amusement and, since I almost never interfered with a teacher's methods, decided to let it go and see where it would lead. One day one of our youngest teachers, who hadn't long been out of a school where gold stars and credits and honors and marks had been the thing all important to work for, came to me greatly troubled and said: "I don't know just what to do about those gilt letters which the children bring out from the shop. Most of the children give them to me to take care of. I have tried to keep track of the number each one has given, but I know I've made mistakes. The queer thing about it is that the children don't seem to care. I tried pinning the letters on the wall, but the wind blew them away." "Not an unnatural ending," I thought.

It was some time before the teachers realized that it was because the work those chil-

dren were doing in the shop was interesting and significant and their achievement of it important to them that the artificial stimulus was superfluous.

People on the outside, often parents of the children, wondered if a school in which children were so happy could be doing any disciplining. And wasn't discipline important? What would happen when children who were always enthusiastic about their work were confronted later by work which was at once arduous and disagreeable and forced to do it?

Two mothers came to me after spending a morning in the school and told me with great delight of the remarkable concentration of the children on their work. "But," they said, "we were troubled by seeing no discipline anywhere." For the moment I was shocked, knowing that they had spent the morning with teachers who had unusual control of children. "Gracious," I said, "were the children disorderly?" "Oh no," they said, "we saw no child out of order, but we saw no discipline." What they missed was the *evidences* of discipline!

A little later I heard an argument going on in the front porch between one of these mothers and her son, which sounded something like this: "Come, dear, Mother is going to stay for lunch. You must wash your hands and be ready when the rest of the children are." "Oh, Mother, why do I have to go now?" "Please hurry, darling, I can't have you late." "But, Mother, I want to show you," etc. At that moment a teacher came along; "Run, boy, and wash your hands," she called in passing, assuming that the boy would obey instantly. The boy tore off to the wash room, and when the mother came to the table, there he was with clean hands, waiting for her. I couldn't resist saying, "Perhaps prompt obedience is one of the evidences of discipline which you were looking for."

A little later the mother was puzzled when her child, who "never touches spinach at

home," ate all that he had on his plate without question. It was another evidence of discipline, but as such it went by unnoticed.

Of course there is all the difference in the world in the ability of grown people to understand and control children. It is a good deal as it is out on a boys' playground. There is the boy who is weak and always a follower. No one would ever think of paying the slightest attention to him if he ever gave a command. Then there is the bully. He controls the smaller boys because they are afraid of him. Always there is the gang leader, chosen and acknowledged by all the boys, and his word is law. It is all quite largely a question of natural leadership.

We hear a good deal these days about children having no respect for authority. The question which always rushes to my mind is this: Is authority always deserving of respect? If a mother brags in her boy's hearing that she was able to break the law and smuggle liquor over from Canada by letting her ten-year-old boy hold it as they drove, should she be surprised when seven years later her boy drinks at the dances he attends and her influence is nil?

I have been in the homes of children who were fine, coöperative, hard-working, obedient children all day long in school, but who behaved so outrageously and disrespectfully in their homes as to make my stay extremely embarrassing. What makes the difference?

In the first place, at school they lived where everything suggested Do. Nothing but the interference in the rights of others suggested Don't. There was something there to do which challenged the very highest effort of everybody in the group. They were too busy and happy in this active living to waste time fussing or quarreling. Besides, the school was theirs and they felt a great pride and responsibility for its welfare. Then they had acquired a poise which came with well-balanced days spent out of doors where the sense of space and calm eliminated fa-

tigue. But, most important of all, they were not constantly trying to conform to an adult's standard of behavior where, in so far as they could see, failure to wipe one's mouth after drinking milk was on a par with stealing another child's toy. They were, instead, developing attitudes of service which later in life would be essential to useful citizenship. There was all the necessary discipline that went with it, a large part of it discipline that came from the inside, which, if you stop to think, is the only kind that is of much value.

These children were forming their own standards of right and wrong. In these days when, for instance, a prominent business man will rise in a large Parents' League meeting and ask for other men in the audience to support him when he tries to prevent his boy's breaking the state law by driving a car when he is only fifteen, I should say that our only hope is to develop in the children themselves right standards of behavior. The same thing is true with standards of work. A teacher can demand a certain quality of work and get it, but I should a thousand times rather see children themselves dissatisfied with poor workmanship and determined to improve it. They often become very harsh judges of their own work.

We can't superimpose our standards upon children. We can't give them our experiences. As far as I am concerned, I am thankful that we can't. On the other hand, we can help children form the habit of thinking things out to logical conclusions, of deciding questions of right and wrong, and of having the courage to stand by what is right at any cost. Professor Hocking in *Human Nature and Its Remaking* says:

> The eternal standard is obscured; hence we do nothing well; we lack sincerity and simplicity; we are suspicious, disunited, flabby; we do not find ourselves; we are not free; unless we recover a working hold on some kind of religious innervation, our democracy will shortly contain little that is worthy to survive.

Our own standards are crumbling about us. Our hope lies in the children.

I believe that there ought to be a sort of preventive discipline. Things for which children should be punished should be for the most part anticipated and prevented. I know that nine tenths of the things for which children are rebuked ought to be overlooked and ignored; the other tenth should be given the importance it deserves.

In all my experience of nearly a quarter of a century with children of all ages in all sorts and conditions of schools I have never used corporal punishment, but I can truthfully say that I should far rather have a child of mine receive a sound spanking every other day than be nagged. Nagging is entirely useless, in addition to being ruinous to the dispositions, to say nothing of the digestions, of the entire family. A good rule to follow might be this. Say "Don't" once for every forty times you let a child Do something. The world would be a better place to live in. Children are not naturally naughty. If they are naughty, it is either because they are tired, ill, under too much restraint, or forced to conform to the fussiness of some grown person who needs a good night's sleep.

I never had more conclusive proof of the importance of environment in its influence on discipline than I once had in my relationship with a near-by public school. Here, instead of a hundred fifty children and an acre and a half of land, was an elementary school of fifteen hundred children without a square foot of playground. When they filed out of the huge brick building, they were at once upon the main street of the city.

One day as I was conversing with the principal, a fine sturdy woman who had been a principal of schools for a good many years and took it very seriously, she confided to me that she was having a great deal of trouble with her fifth- and sixth-grade boys. "They have killed off three women teachers, and now I am getting in a man who, if

need be, can use brute force," she said. I found that there were all together a hundred fifty boys, just the population of our own school. Impulsively I asked: "Oh, will you let me have them? You see, our children have a half-holiday every Wednesday afternoon, and there stands our whole place unused. Can't you send them over at three o'clock every Wednesday afternoon to stay until supper time?" I wish you might have seen the mixture of kind tolerance and utter incredulity on her face when she looked at me and said: "Why, my dear woman, you don't know what you are asking! Don't you know that, if you give these boys an inch, they will take a mile?" I think I finally convinced her that they were entitled to more than an inch. Anyway, the long and short of it was that she let them come, bless her.

Several of my teachers came to me and argued with me against the idea. Some of them were naturally worried for fear the work in the open bungalows might be destroyed. The Frenchman asked me if I didn't think it would be safer all around if he stayed to help me control them. But even though I may have had some wavering moments, I realized that of course, if I expected it to succeed, I must keep my faith in the idea.

On the following Wednesday, having sent every teacher and child home, I sat at my office window and waited for the mob to arrive. I found myself saying: "Brute force? I wonder!"

I needn't have watched. I heard them coming when they were still two blocks away. I met them at the front gate and asked: "Have you by any chance a gang leader? Is there a boss of your gang?" There was indeed, and they pushed him forward. I recognized him as the boy whose name I was told had been most often on the police roll. I then explained to him, the other boys listening with a respectful hush (respect, I

mean, for their boss), that it had seemed to me a great pity that this place should stand idle on Wednesday afternoons, when it was such a fine place for boys to play in, and that I much preferred having it used. I told them that the outdoor gymnasium was theirs to use as they wished and that there was no objection to their using the basket balls. I showed them a pile of soft wood which I had had dumped at the corner of the fence and told them that they might use the hammers and nails and saws which I had left there. I showed them where our boys played baseball, and I took them out to the orchard, full of climbable trees. I even suggested as a climax their bringing their sneakers the next time and playing about over the roofs of the buildings. Then I said, "I want you to have a good time; use everything, but please keep out of the schoolrooms because those belong to the children and some of the things which they think are very important might accidentally be injured."

I never enjoyed anything more in my life. When I couldn't stand it indoors any longer, I went out and played with them. One day as we sat on the steps watching a baseball game, one of the worst little toughs in the lot left me, dashed out the front gate, and when he came back inconspicuously thrust into my hand a very sticky lollipop. "It's more fun when you can suck suckers," he said.

The boys came every Wednesday for the rest of the year, and during all that time not a th ng was injured or stolen. A window or two was broken with baseballs and paid for without any demand from me. Nobody had used "brute force," and most of the time these boys weren't even supervised.

The following winter at Christmas time I didn't have to hire any men to help put the ornaments on the Christmas tree.

Given a place and an opportunity for play, plus a faith quietly assumed that a boy will make the most of it, the result is almost invariably a good spirit and good behavior.

X

WE kept on growing until we seemed to be fairly bursting from our bungalows. Our girls had reached the eighth grade, and we had all together a family of a hundred seventy. Something must be done. Even guests, instead of visiting the school, wandered about restlessly looking for a place where we might tuck away a ninth grade the following year. "What next?" was the all-important question. It was hardly the thing to say to parents, "Now we have given your children the finest beginnings in education we know anything about, and we hope that you will be able to continue their education elsewhere." I leave you to imagine, too, what such a plan would have done to our experiment. It would have been vague and absolutely worthless. Our idea was eventually to carry both boys and girls on together to college, but for years we must keep that absolutely to ourselves. Our community was not ready for it. The school had grown a year at a time; and while some of us were already looking very far ahead, this seemed to be the logical development. Teachers, trustees, and friends of the school had scoured the country about looking for a place suitable for a girls' upper school, but nothing which we found seemed at all adequate.

One morning a wonderful thing happened. I was sitting in my office, thinking of the hopelessness of some of the places which we had looked at, when a woman who was one of the original committee for the school came in. She was a woman of great charm and a beautiful spirit, and I knew the minute I looked at her that she had something very unusual to tell me. I was hardly prepared for what she said. She asked me if I remembered, years ago when the school was in its infancy, lunching with her at her country home and if I remembered telling her that

of all places I had ever seen her sixty-acre farm seemed ideal for a school. She went on to say that, although no one knew it, she and her husband had just come to the conclusion that it was best to sell their estate, and she wanted me to be the first one to know it. I must have seemed to her utterly stupid and ungrateful, but the chance suddenly to acquire the most perfect spot in the vicinity for our school expansion rendered me quite inarticulate.

It was a beautiful estate with a home which had been built by true home lovers. On that next morning when we drove out to see it, it stood smothered in apple blossoms. The farm lay on the slope of a hill overlooking almost the only distant view which the city afforded. There were scattered about over it large barns in perfect repair, carriage sheds, and a little farmhouse in which lived the farmer and his wife. There were a great apple orchard, large trees, fields of grain, and a tiny brook winding its way down to two enchanting ponds.　Near the house were two formal gardens, bordered with iris, hemmed in by lilacs, white and purple, and filled with every sort of perennial.　Almost best of all, there was at the entrance of the estate a little, very old, stone house, banked with lilacs and forsythias, having in its gardens flowers and herbs which might have been growing there for nearly a century.

"What a paradise for children," I thought. But on second thought, "What a lot to be done before we could ever pick up our school bodily and transplant it to this heavenly spot!"

In the first place, there were the trustees to be convinced.　I was really afraid that something might happen to the precious plan if I brought it before them at a meeting.　I therefore, within twenty-four hours, invited each trustee out in turn to tell him about it individually.　Within a few days we had a faculty-trustee supper, a very jolly one. Every one was enthusiastic over the plan,

and within a week the trustees had underwritten the property.　I didn't find out until some time afterward that the property had been very heavily mortgaged and that ten men had signed a very large note at the bank to make the purchase possible.

This was a serious mistake because at that time, while the enthusiasm was at its height and the demand insistent, it would have been comparatively easy to raise money.　It is always vastly easier to raise money for a growing concern when enthusiasm runs high than it is to get people to give money later to pay off a debt or a deficit.　Besides this, several of the men had no business to be asked to sign such a note.　They were not financially able to assume such a responsibility.

In any event, however, a great faith was shown by these trustees who made it possible for us to have the farm.　A few years after the purchase, when the value of the property had a great deal more than doubled, it looked as though, after all, it hadn't been a bad stroke of business.

The next fall, on the opening day, about forty little girls of the eighth and ninth grades left the old school and the younger children and became hostesses for the opening day in the hall of the beautiful home which was to be their school home until they were ready for college.

We set about remodeling buildings, making a classroom and a shop out of a carriage house and garage and a studio out of a barn, with box stalls converted into a classroom, the hay loft into a crafts room, and with a great stone fireplace to make it all artistic and homelike.

Down near the little ponds we built an outdoor, wooden platform without any shelter. This was to be used all the year round as an out-of-door gymnasium. Although I suggested it because we had no money with which to build a gymnasium, I never want to have another school without one. It was

easily shoveled in snow time, and there was scarcely a day in the year when it wasn't being used pretty constantly all day long. It was a perfect place for folk dancing, assemblies, out-of-door plays and pageants, daily vigorous setting-up exercises, basket ball, etc.

A confused mixture of memories comes to me concerning the first year; they aren't all of apple blossoms and sunshine. Finding teachers who had been specializing in subjects and getting them to believe that there were other things in the long day's living of equal importance was the most difficult task of the first year. Concern lest the buzzer which defined the length of classes should be of prime importance was expressed. What crimes have been committed in the way of breaking up sustained thinking and concentration of attention by the ringing of buzzers in classrooms! And yet we succeeded in getting one or two teachers who caught the spirit and the essence of what the girls had brought with them into the high school and which they were loath to lose.

There were days when the very men who had decided upon the new school were in despair over the expense which had of necessity been involved by running this big plant, with teachers enough for a large high school, for our small group of eighth- and ninth-grade girls. It would be some time before we could expect to fill it up from our lower school, and yet we couldn't go on one step at a time as we had previously done. We must have teachers for nearly all our high school subjects. The new teachers, who hadn't grown up with the school, needed an infinite amount of attention, education, and constant optimism provided them.

The transportation question didn't solve itself. Parents were dubious about the whole thing. There were months together when it would have taken very little to cause the abrupt withdrawal of many of the girls, and that would have killed the school. Was

there not within decent distance of home schools which many of the mothers had attended and which they knew would prepare their girls to pass college entrance examinations? There was another grave doubt in parents' minds of our being able to reach the farm at all on very snowy mornings. Many days might be lost during the winter. Of course, one would occasionally hear something like this, but it wasn't often, "My girl might miss half the winter and still be the gainer in such a school."

Well I remember when the first test came. It was in November, and we awoke one morning to a raging blizzard. No street cars had been running on Main Street since midnight. Parents began calling up at seven thirty to ask if there would be any school at all. "Of course there will," we answered, and we rushed out between calls to shovel out the bungalows. There was little question about the Lower School, for we had lived through many blizzards there and thrived on them. My answer to parents of the Upper School was, "Send the girls out as far as the old school anyway, and we'll see." Well I knew how many people were waiting to say, "I told you so." If it was humanly possible to avoid it, I didn't mean to give them the chance.

Only about ten minutes late, the great busses full of children arrived, and the younger ones piled out. I started to get in with the older girls when I was met by the downright refusal of the drivers to go any farther. Out we all got. Even the teachers said, "Surely you are not going to attempt that trip." We took the drivers inside, warmed them up with coffee and doughnuts until they became fairly good-natured. We held the two limousines which had brought the kindergarten babies, and in fifteen minutes we were ready to start. Some of the Lower School teachers tell me that they remember very vividly just how I looked in boots, wading in snow up to my knees,

as with the help of some of the big boys and several sympathetic men on the street I pushed the huge bus around the corner. Anyway we made it. It was fun to answer the phone calls of anxious business men from their offices as they called up to find out what we were going to do in the face of the terrible blizzard and to tell them that we had arrived and were already hard at work. We arrived forty minutes late, to be sure, but we conducted school as usual for the rest of the day, which is more than many of the public schools did, and one of our questions was settled for always.

The demands of the Lower School four miles away were heavy that year and, more often than I like, I remember being halfway between the two schools. I can recall days when I had times of great depression, when it would have been very unsafe for me to meet trustees or parents or teachers. At such times I would beg the teachers to let me teach their classes, and things would somehow straighten themselves out. No one could lose heart after working with those children.

But as I look back now, the times I remember best are the long, quiet evenings after everyone had gone, when I roamed about over the farm. The distance to the far horizon seemed limitless. In that space and silence I got my real perspective on the venture, and dreams for the future were all-absorbing and very sure. There was, above all, a deep abiding joy in the development which overcame any doubt or fear.

XI

I SHALL not soon forget the faculty meeting in the spring when I proposed moving out all the children to the farm amd selling the old place. The teachers all had a great deal of sentiment for this school home which we had fought, bled, and almost died to keep. But, as I have told you before, they were a very remarkable and creative group of people. They seized upon the idea and grappled with it, and before we left that night they had already begun in their own minds a campaign to convince parents.

Four miles farther out in the country was all very well for older girls who could stand the trip. When I spoke about our plan to one of the trustees, his response was anything but encouraging. To have proposed the thing outright to the patrons of the school would have been fatal. But these teachers went about quietly among the parents of their pupils, saying a word here and another word there, managing in some magic way to get every mother out to the farm. Some of them gave teas out there for mothers and children. An Easter egg hunt was planned by the older girls for the little children of the school in the gardens, and all the mothers were invited. The first-grade teacher invited the mothers of her pupils to go out with her in the children's school bus one afternoon in May, when the country was irresistible. Nobody realized until some time afterward that the big school bus had been used so that mothers would feel safer in the fall about letting their children ride in it. One of our teachers, who was our bird expert, took groups of boys and girls out there in the early mornings, and the sixth-grade teacher asked if she might move her whole class out there for the spring term and live in the garage, which we had made into an attractive, sunny schoolroom. Gardens were started by the children. The hay barns and the little calves made the appeal

that they do to all children. Finally we gave a beautiful spring festival, which was attended by practically every parent in the school and many friends besides.

Among our parents was an architect who had two children in the school. He lived out near this farm and had a real appreciation of what the country was doing for his children. I found him very sympathetic when I went to him to propose my plan for building a little village for the Lower School. Of course, the idea was a natural one, since in a sense that was what we had at the old school. But when I told him that I wanted to build in the large orchard a lot of little houses which should constitute a Primary Village, that the little houses should be built for children and should be grouped around a village green as houses were in New England, and that each should contain one or possibly two families of children, he was thrilled with the idea. He had a great deal of imagination and loved children, qualities which made him the ideal architect for us. The very next night he met all the primary teachers at supper, and each teacher told him just what she most wanted in her own little building.

Away he went and made the most enchanting plans you ever saw. In addition to these he made lovely water-color sketches. With these plans I met the trustees and later all the parents of the school at two meetings, which were called very hastily. You must remember that the real work of convincing them had been done thoroughly by the teachers, and these plans, making the thing very attractive and definite, did the rest.

In all the years of the school I had never seen the enthusiasm so high. The desire for the little Primary Village set in an apple orchard in the midst of a great farm became a demand. So afraid were these parents that the thing might not come to pass that one Sunday morning a dozen enthusiastic fathers and mothers came out to the school for lists of patrons, and during that day and

the next they got the signatures of all the parents in the school, expressing their desire to see that the fulfillment of the plan was secured. In addition, these people got the signatures of a great many influential men of the city who had no children in the school but were interested in the thing as a civic venture.

Out at the farm a week later, an informal supper was given to all the patrons of the school. It wasn't difficult then to launch a financial drive for $100,000. The idea had already been sold. Nor was it difficult to get it, which we did, within $10,000, before July first. There were many men in the city who thought that it would have been just as easy to raise twice that amount, especially if it had been put through before the big university drive for fifty times that amount. But although we followed close in their wake, we raised the amount we went out for, and practically all of it from our own patrons. The Primary Village was assured.

That summer I lived in the old house which held so many happy memories and day by day heard crashing about my ears the green bungalows as the indifferent wrecking company tore them to pieces. As they ruthlessly pried them apart I shivered. Would life in the new environment ever be as complete as this had been? When I grew too apprehensive, I rushed out to the farm where the new dream was coming true. There were always many details to be decided upon. I went about over the buildings anxiously, with my plans clutched in my hand, to see if the lower grade teachers' little shops, with lofts overhead where the children could keep the lumber, were being built; if the tiny kitchen, which the teacher who loved to cook would infinitely prefer to a shop, was really materializing. Oh, it was a very thrilling summer, and the happiest I have ever known.

But it was nothing to the ecstatic joy of the opening days when the children came out, all of them, to live in the little village among the apple trees. Multiply the happiness which one child gets when he arrives on a farm by one hundred fifty, and you can come somewhere near catching the enthusiasm which existed. Add to that the knowledge that the farm was theirs for their very own, and even then, because you are grown up and have become accustomed to the artificiality which surrounds you and the complicated living which you now demand, you will fall far short of a real understanding of the complete satisfaction which was theirs.

Then indeed we really began to live. Surely responsibilities will never be lacking here, I thought. Work will always be purposeful, and there will be plenty to go around. The raising of chickens began to be a serious business. Eggs were needed for the school. Gardens in which could actually be raised enough tomatoes and corn and potatoes for our school lunches for a hundred fifty children assumed importance accordingly. One day I met a radiant little girl of six who stopped me and said, "Doesn't this remind you of 'This place is so full of a number of things that I'm sure we should all be as happy as kings'?"

If I haven't said as much as you think I should have of subject matter and curriculum, it is not because I don't consider the relation of academic work to the art of living on a farm of tremendous importance, but because other educators have written convincingly about subject matter. Eugene Smith in his book *Education Moves Ahead* has reached large numbers of parents as well as teachers. Besides, I have given talks for so many years to teachers, on curriculum making, reading, writing, and arithmetic, that I wanted to write here about a phase of education which seems to me all-important and which might be more easily overlooked. Teachers, instead of doing their own thinking, are altogether too prone to take courses from anybody who will supply them on

"methods of teaching the subjects." Some of them seem to me to have gone methodology mad. Methods are after all only the means to the end. So often the end becomes utterly swallowed up and completely lost in the craze for methods. Besides, the very people who should be doing the thinking are following the line of least resistance and asking some teachers' college to do it for them. Often these methods are manufactured to order by theorists who have never had or taught a child in their lives.

However, I will say for those who are rightfully interested in the subject end of the work that we were probably more conscientious than most schools, for the very reason that we were trying to prove that a school may live as fully as we were doing and, really because of it, become farther advanced than most schools in the academic work of the school. The standard tests, in fact every test which had been devised, had been tried on these children. They tested "up to grade," although they were over a year younger than the average school age, and every class but one in the elementary school tested in reading two years above grade. We could see no reason why they shouldn't. Health and happiness, interest and purpose in work, the life out of doors eliminated much of the fatigue and waste of time which handicaps progress in the average school.

XII

FROM the beginning we had been educating with a view to stimulating creative imagination, on the one hand, and finding work which was meaningful and needed to be done, on the other. This was not difficult in the Lower School, where the children belonged to one teacher. What would happen when these children fell into the hands of teachers of subjects — Latin, algebra, physics, history, athletics?

Our answer was this. We would not let go of our "free period," which had meant everything to us in the Lower School. In the Upper School the period after lunch became, instead of a "free period," a "hobby hour."

At the entrance to the driveway of our sixty-acre farm, set a little way back from the road, stood, as I have said, a very old, little, gray stone house. It had been used of late years by the servants and once as a museum

by the children who used to live on this estate. Like many little houses of the period, it
admitted the minimum of light and sunshine.
But about it were lilac bushes which had become trees, old apple trees, and a garden
which must have dated back many years,
with herbs and roses that were better known
to our grandmothers.

As if by magic this little house appeared
in answer to our question. Had not the girls
reached the age when home-making instincts
came to the front? To what better use could
the house ever be put? The same friend
who gave to us practically everything which
had made our school living in the new environment full and worth while, our library,
our gardens, our athletic field and tennis
courts, our physics laboratory, and later a
large part of our junior high school, made it
possible to carry out here in the little stone
house one of our most valuable projects.
Always he wished to remain unknown as a
benefactor, but the girls knew that somebody

had made a wonderful dream come true for
them.

I wish you would let one or two of the
girls' letters tell you better than I can how
this house with its crying demand to be used
as a part of our school gave us a real motive
for the most meaningful kind of work which
one could possibly find for girls.

Dear Parrain:

Which I am going to call you until you tell us your
name. Were you ever suddenly and unexpectedly
told that you were to have something which you had
always wanted but always considered impossible?
Perhaps if you have, you can imagine the way we
felt when, one rest hour, Miss —— mysteriously
called us into her office and told us that we were to
have the little Stone House, all for our very own!

You really should have been there. Miss ——'s
office came very near losing its roof, but she very
effectually quieted us by asking if anybody could
read plans! Then she produced, not one plan, but a
pile of plans — one for each of us! You see the very
nicest architect, we think, in the city has some children in the Lower School, and he happens to be, as
of course any right-minded person would be, crazy

about the school. So that he offered his services *perfectly free* and sent out enough plans of the house, as it looked then, for each of us to have one! We all took them home and discussed, by ourselves, the possibilities. Then we had a second meeting in which we each told what we thought would improve the house.

One fine morning, our architect came out to see us. That was most exciting. We all grouped around him in the big living room and several chosen spokesmen told him of our ideas, to which he listened carefully and, if some of our ideas were rather inappropriate, architecturally or otherwise, telling us tactfully why. A few days later he sent us our second plans, which were very thrilling and which included our suggestions. Three pages! One showing the first floor, the next the second floor, and the third the fireplace, which we had decided was absolutely essential for our living room. Imagine a poor little house without one!

Perhaps you would like to know what we are planning to use the house for. It is to be our playhouse, only our idea of a playhouse is one in which we can play house. Just think of a playhouse with a real, I almost said live, kitchen in which we could get supper; a real living room such as we would have at home, only, of course, smaller and very much cozier. Wouldn't it be fun to give a tea, all by ourselves, which we would serve in our living room! But I've forgotten our two little bedrooms that we are going to have

upstairs! *We* ourselves can spend nights in them, and then our tiny kitchen would be very convenient. Oh, I forgot to mention our cellar. We have a cellar in our house, too.

We formed ourselves into four different groups. The first consisted of girls who were most interested in domestic science because they are having their second year of cooking, and they were to have charge of the kitchen. Interior decoration in a kitchen sounds rather unusual, doesn't it? Nevertheless it is very important. It will be one of our homiest rooms. The second and third groups of girls each have a bedroom to furnish. Last, but not by any means least, as it consists of my class, is the group which has charge of the living room. The most interesting part of the home, we think, but there are some who don't agree with us.

It took us so long to get our bids, which are, you know, a rather important part, that there was some question, a very small one, so small that some of us did not even see it, as to whether we could remodel this spring or not. We finally did have to compromise. We are remodeling this spring, but we won't furnish the house, literally, that is, until next fall.

We decided that it would be a great help if we had a budget to go on. It would teach us to economize. Usually when you are building you have to. It has been great fun getting our bids and figuring up just how much we shall spend on what.

As the younger girls have not come in on this at all we thought it would be nice to give the garden to them to make. No home, you know, is complete without one. This is going to be the loveliest you ever saw, I know.

Now, Parrain, if we only knew who you were, just think how nice it would be. You would be invited to spend the night in our house. We should get you the most delicious meals you ever tasted. Doesn't that tempt you? And you know anybody that sleeps in either of these rooms sleeps twice as well as he does at home! You could sit in front of a crackling fire in our tiny living room. Just think how nice it would be for us if you would only let us know who you are! Please do, because, you know, we shall be so disappointed if you don't come to spend the night in our little Stone House some time, very soon, after it is finished.

With much curiosity and much more gratitude,

E. C.

My dear Miss E. C:

"Parrain" has read with great interest and pleasure your letter, my interest centering upon the loving service of you and your associates in the transformation of the little, old, stone house into a practical playhouse for little mothers of the future. My pleasure is due to a successful application of a little money

and the realization of a dream. I thank you for your vivid description of the details.

Your curiosity to ascertain an identity is only human. Perhaps you remember the thrills that Santa Claus, as a mystery, gave you and also remember that you lost something when the mystery was revealed. I think you will find that the thrills will only return when you embody the spirit of Santa Claus in your own person. I should like to suggest that this mystery be handed down to each succeeding generation of little mistresses of the "Little Stone House," and also at the beginning of each school year you might have a "Daddy Long Legs Day" and thus initiate the new mistresses to their domain.

I should like to suggest a thought in this connection that might be worthy of perpetuation. It's the thinking of good things to do, and doing them, that makes life worth while; and I might add to that, with self-effacement always.

Wishing you all happiness in your work and play, I beg still to remain, your mysterious

Parrain

Dear Mr. Architect:

We cannot thank you enough for the dandy blueprints you made for us of our little stone house! We have put them into use and have spent a deal of time at the place making our plans. There are a few changes that we want to make in the house itself; one of them is to have a fireplace put in the living room; we don't know whether there is a flue anywhere, and we would like to consult you about that. We also thought of moving the wall between the kitchen and the living room so as to make more room in the latter. If we do that, we want the partition between the kitchen and the pantry knocked out to make the kitchen look bigger and to let more light into the pantry.

Upstairs we think it will be necessary to separate the two bedrooms so that we won't have to go through one to get to the other.

We are going to do the rest all by ourselves, the painting and furnishing and so forth, but we should appreciate immensely a visit from you to talk over the carpentry end of it. Any time that is convenient for you to come out to our country home, we will be very glad to see you.

We are sending you some drawings with this letter which will help explain what we hope we can do. I am very much afraid you will have to use your imagination on the upstairs plan to understand it fully.

You don't know how much your services have been to us and how indispensable you are to our school, for we couldn't have gotten along without you.

Sincerely yours,

K. C.

A year and a half later.

Dear Parrain:

So much has happened since we last wrote you!

The "Little Stone House" no longer stands cold and lonely by the gate, but pink flowers peeping through ruffled curtains, which we made ourselves, are the first welcome to everyone who comes to our school.

Of course, the first thing we did in furnishing the house was to plan just what and how we wanted the most important pieces of furniture. What thought over whether a little spindled rocking chair would be better in this or that corner than a settee with a blue pillow upon it!

But the best part was carrying out that which we planned. You would have been surprised if you had happened to go by an antique shop to see some of us rushing out with a long mirror in one hand and a precious candlestick under the other arm. Beds, chairs, and tables poured into the little house; some perhaps a little dull and shabby, only to come forth again freshly painted and designed.

If you could have come to see us any afternoon right after lunch last spring, we are sure you would never have seen more busy girls. Some of us would have been hemming and sewing ruffles on curtains. Under the trees some would be scraping and painting quaint chairs and bureaus which had been chosen with great care for especially cosy nooks where they would just fit. Then others would have been weaving bewitching colors into round pink and applegreen rag rugs for the bedrooms and a big blue homey one for the living room.

Of course, we could hardly wait until it was all finished so that we could have a real house warming party of all the "Upper School." So we set a date and everyone excitingly finished up a few last tasks and planned merrily of the good times to come.

And was our first party a success? It couldn't have been anything else. We stayed one night after school and coasted and skated until dark, but, oh, the very nicest part was afterwards, when we were all so cold and starved, to have a house of our very own in which to eat our supper, which some of us cooked — in front of our cheery little fireplace.

So you see someone is always busy and happy there. Not many days pass when some group of girls is not showing, by inviting mothers to lunch or a tea or a picnic, how much we really love our own "Little Stone House." We all feel that it is almost the most important part of our school.

Won't you, even now, let us know who you are and let us show you, ourselves, all the attractive details that mean so much to us?

President of The Little Stone House Club

The remodeling of this little house offered every kind of opportunity for purposeful and creative work, from whitewashing the cellar and building closets for jellies and jams, from building up cupboards and shelves and broom closets in the kitchen, consulting plumbers about sinks, and choosing all the shiny kitchen utensils, from buying, after much shopping, china which was "just what we wanted" for the dining room and painting the floors to working on two teams and rivaling each other in furnishing the two little bedrooms, which had been made most attractive by the introduction of little dormer windows. We spent much time in studying the types of furniture, wall paper, etc., of a hundred years ago, and even to making our own rag and pulled rugs we were consistent. An account was opened at the bank, and the girls, with a finance committee of their own, worked entirely within the budget which they set for themselves. In furnishing this little house they came upon the same questions of relative values of purchases which they are some day going to meet in furnishing their own homes. And many of these girls were wealthy girls who had none too good a sense of money values.

Landscaping about the little house gave a chance for those especially gifted in this line to work out their own designs and plans.

All in all, I never, before or since, have run across anything which has proved to be so valuable a project in education.

XIII

THERE was a thing which now began to happen, of which even those of us that were closest at hand were only dimly perceptive.

During all these years we had been sending our boys away at the end of the sixth grade to the only boys' upper private school in the city. All the private schools had been feeding this school for years. It was an excellent school of the conservative type, patterned after the English schools. There were head masters and masters. Academic subjects were stressed. The classics were thoroughly taught. There had been no science or manual training included in the curriculum until within a year or two of this time. But the reputation of the pupils for passing college entrance examinations was excellent. What was more to the point, our boys' fathers had attended this school, and their elder brothers were there. It was easy to assume that our boys were looking forward with great eagerness to following their example.

One morning early in the spring one of our mothers stopped me as I was making my rounds over the farm and asked me if I realized that some of our boys were really dreading the thought of leaving us to go to ——. "Why, that is quite impossible," I said, thinking of their new $50,000 gymnasium, with its artificial skating rink, of their reputation in athletics, for which boys care so much, and of their football coach. "Aren't they counting the days until they get there?" I said. "Well, my boy isn't," she answered. "I don't think even you have any conception of the loyalty these boys have for their school."

I did some pretty rapid thinking. Of course that would complete our project as we had originally planned it, and we could take boys and girls all the way to college. Under the conditions of life as they exist

to-day, coeducation is more than normal; it is necessary. We had been ready for it for some time, but it had seemed the part of wisdom to coöperate with this school and not attempt to compete with it until we were much stronger. The city wasn't ready for the development of a private coeducational school. If we had been at all precipitate, we should have lost the confidence of people when we needed it most. We had been moving pretty rapidly in ten years. First we had left the little cottage and bought the beautiful estate; to that, each year, we made additions; then we had purchased the farm six miles from the city and established the beginnings of an Upper School for girls, with a new high school faculty; then we had picked up the entire Lower School bodily, kindergarten and all, moved them out, and built for them a Primary Village. Now we were considering the possibility of establishing a junior high school or an intermediate school for boys and girls for sixth, seventh,

and eighth grades, with a ninth grade to follow the next year. Of course it was the
logical thing to do, to meet the issue when the
demand came. It was just what we had
done in each other case. But was it a
demand? I determined to find out.

First I decided to talk it all over with a
group of fathers and mothers who were most
concerned. We sat before the fire one evening a little later, and I found that they
seemed to be very heartily in favor of it.
But the boys themselves? They were the
ones, after all, to be considered. Wasn't this
a children's school?

The very next morning I invited into my
office the boys and girls who would be concerned in the plan. Without a preliminary
discussion, except to paint in rather more
rosy colors than was necessary the advantages
of the other school, I asked them how they
would like to stay and continue their schooling on the farm. The Upper School classes
had to stop work during the resounding

"yeas" that followed. I then told them
that the whole thing would be in their hands.
I told them that I had persuaded hard-
headed business men to buy the farm for
us, that I had helped the teachers persuade
all the mothers and fathers to send the children out there, that the parents of the school
had raised nearly a hundred thousand dollars to make it all possible, and that even
if I wanted to, I probably couldn't persuade
them within a year to erect a new intermediate school for them.

"But," I said, "I'll tell you what I will
do. I will let you convince the parents.
If you will invite all the parents of the school
out to supper a week or ten days from to-
night and if, without any help from me or
the teachers, you will, after supper, conduct
a meeting with your own chairman and
speakers and if you can (I am afraid I said)
sell them the idea, I think the school will
be yours."

Such a ten days as followed! Interest in

work seemed to have become a passion. The regular work of the shop was entirely turned over to meet the insistent demands for a model of a building, an upright structure which would "show people who couldn't understand plans so well." The art work changed from Egyptian design to mechanical drawings, floor plans, landscape gardening, and most alluring water-colored sketches. On entering an English class you would find a heated debate going on: "*Resolved*, that a farm is the place for both boys and girls." Work everywhere seemed to have taken on a new significance.

At last the evening arrived. It was one of the worst nights I have ever known. Rain came down in torrents. Nothing dampened the spirits or the confidence of these boys and girls. By six thirty over a hundred mothers and fathers were sitting at the tables in our large dining room and being waited upon by the children. It was a very democratic gathering, for we had a very

democratic school. Sitting beside a man who might have written a check large enough to swing the whole thing was a little sewing woman who was working nights to keep her child in the school.

It was a very gay party. I stopped the waiter at my table and said to him, "Who are the debaters to-night?" and he answered as quick as a flash: "Well, you see, Miss ——, we are not exactly debaters; we're convincers. We've got to win." "Nothing can prevent it," I thought.

After the supper the boys and girls who were to decide the fate of the new intermediate school went up and sat down on the rug in front of the fire, and the chairman, a boy of eleven, announced the meeting. One after another of those boys and girls stood up and talked to the group of assembled parents as though their lives depended upon it. For that reason and because they had formed the habit of attacking a hard task with courage and determination, they talked well.

Then the meeting was thrown open to the house, and the chairman urged everybody to take part. We had never before had such a general participation in a discussion. Some of the best known doctors in the city took part. The architect who had been asked by the children to consult with them about their plans was there and entered into the discussion. A state senator made a rousing speech. So high was the final enthusiasm that a dignified president of one of our large banks jumped into his chair and, waving his napkin in the air, led in three cheers for the new school. He then asked for a standing vote of all present. Only four or five people in the room remained seated. The children were elated by receiving at that moment a special delivery letter from one of the members of the board who could not be present, expressing his great interest and belief in the plan.

After that meeting can you imagine our not going ahead with plans? It had been a

most thrilling party. On the way out, however, one of the trustees who had voted against it said to me with considerable gravity: "It is easy to live out here on this beautiful farm and think of things to do next. I am heartily in favor of the plan, but how are we going to finance it?" He was absolutely right. It had been amazing to me that more people hadn't felt the same way. But it was worth something to us to have found the right thing to do. Ways and means should follow. Without quite realizing just what it meant, I answered, "The responsibility for raising the funds this time should be mine, and I'll take it."

I had never before asked anybody for money, and I must say that it was with considerable dread that I set about raising $27,000, which was the sum estimated for the very simple structure together with its tiny cottage. I had several interesting interviews with men from whom I received nothing. I had not one unpleasant interview.

At the end of eight days $24,000 had been pledged and, what is more, a very keen interest aroused in the success of the plan. This was in April. In the fall of that year the school building stood, tiny cottage and all, exactly as the children who had been "convincers" on the night of their party had planned it.

What I want you to realize is that the dramatic success of this enterprise was not an accident, but was a natural result in a school where from the very beginning we had held consistently to our belief that children must be led to see the real significance of work and through that to think for themselves, to have the courage of their convictions and be able to express them clearly and convincingly, to take responsibilities, and to put things through. These children had been building their own *school* from the time they set foot in it. What more natural than that they should plan a *school building* to hold their school?

This building contained two large sunny classrooms, each with a large fireplace, low windows swinging out, and broad window seats. The alcoves, bookcases, and the walls were a soft gray, with bright colors brought in by gay Indian rugs and bright curtains and pillows. They were very simply and inexpensively furnished with tables and chairs which the children stained. Upstairs were an open-air classroom and a perfectly equipped science laboratory, which were a gift. Of course we had a boys' club room and a little girls' cottage, which gave the girls a strong motive for work in their free-time period. There were the walls to stain and furniture to make. But the room they loved best was the tiny kitchen. Buying the gay dishes and the shining tinware was such fun and incidentally a very valuable experience. A large athletic field, also a gift, helped perfect the immediate environment for the school.

The opening, a harvest party, was very

impressive, beginning with a dignified processional of the girls and boys, their books held tightly under their arms, singing as they walked, their heads held high, into the school of their own making.

XIV

I HAVE said a great deal about environment, especially with reference to the opportunity it provided for meaningful work and service. But in these days when the business of living is stressed out of all proportion to the art of living, I wanted to be sure that among other experiences, children were storing up many beautiful impressions. The things you remember best about your childhood are not the things you learned in school, nor the things which your parents thought you would remember, but often they are small and very insignificant details. Perhaps you remember being held in your father's arms under a great tree where he rushed with you for shelter from a sudden shower, and the smell of the rain on parched leaves brings it back to you to this day. Or you may remember the smell of a certain house in the country where you often visited in the summer. Nearly always your strongest memories are of sights or smells or sounds.

I was fortunate enough to have a father who, although he was a very busy lawyer, always found time, almost from the moment I was able to walk, to take me for walks in the woods. He knew where to look for arbutus under the snow and later for the tiny, white, fragrant violets which grew near the brook. In the fall, on this same walk, he was the first to find the cardinal flower and the lovely blue gentian. Always he was looking to discover some new kind of moss or fern. I remember how silent he became from the moment he entered the woods. He knew the birds by their notes and taught me to recognize the songs of the veery and the hermit thrush long before I went to school.

But the thing I remember best was the beauty which he seemed so often to find in very little things, a graceful sedge, the gleam of a shining clump of hepaticas in the dead leaves, the color of a bit of lichen against the gray of a beech tree. It was as though he seemed to realize that I was too little to appreciate yet the glory of a great sunset or a distant view.

The priceless thing which this did for me was not only to make me very observant, but to keep me constantly on the lookout for beauty in little, common things. There is nothing in the world which I would exchange for it.

How to bring anything at all like this to little children in school was a question I often asked myself. And where else was there a chance for it in this busy world of to-day? There seemed to me but two things to do: first, to surround children with beauty in its natural form, giving them the most simple and beautiful out-of-door setting, close to nature and, second, to give them teachers who themselves appreciated beauty enough so that they knew how to let children absorb and feel it without being talked to too much about it.

One day a little kindergarten child of four happened, on one of their walks, to glance straight up and found herself looking directly into the face of a huge sunflower blossom. She remained transfixed. Several of the children stumbled over her. Her teacher discovered her, her face radiant, and heard her murmuring to herself, "So pretty, so pretty." This wasn't on the program of the morning walk, but I rejoiced to see the kindergarten teacher stop with the little girl and wait without a word till the baby had her fill of the beautiful yellow against the bluest of skies. Later, in the classroom, she *didn't say:* "Here, dear, is some nice yellow and blue chalk. Won't you make me a picture showing just how the sunflower looked?"

A long, silent walk across the fields and down by the brook after the magical, first, soft fall of snow; singing out in the gardens at sunset; swinging beneath an apple tree in full bloom; walking at quiet time down the path through the cherry blossoms to the

little summer house; Christmas carol singing out among the evergreen trees in the park after a lovely snowstorm; reading "Oh, to be in England" down by the ponds when April was "there"; lying and meditating under the trees at rest hour; these were some of the ways in which we tried to let the beauty of out of doors come into our very souls, hoping thus to build up a resistance to the artificialities of modern complicated living.

One day we had as one of our many guests Dr. O. DeCroly of Belgium. In an article which he wrote later for *L'Ère Nouvelle*, he expresses his delight in the natural beauty of our surroundings. He begins an article descriptive of the school in this way:

Le Rêve Entrevu

Une journée à " —— School"

Chez le Professor John Dewey

Dans le petit bureau de la Columbia University, encombré de livres de tous les temps et de tous les pays, où le plus grand philosophe d'Amérique nous avait si aimablement reçus, nous discutions des méthodes d'éducation. Le maître, dont les yeux rieurs brillaient d'une fine ironie, s'interposa avec douceur et dit très simplement: "Il n'y a qu'une méthode: celle de la vie! Allez à —— School. Peut-être que vous l'y trouverez!"

Et nous y sommes allés, sans parti pris, en toute simplicité' comme il sied lorsqu'on cherche avant tout la vérité.

L'arrivée

Ce fut par un matin glorieux. La terre encore lourde de sommeil s'étirait dans la brume mauve de sa respiration. Les arbres, vivifiés par les sèves printanières, frissonnaient d'aise de se sentir si jeunes et, dans l'air parfumé, les oiseaux annonçaient le gai réveil d'un jour superbe.

L'auto stoppe devant le perron d'une spacieuse maison, construite en bois sombre et que la vigne vierge assaille de toutes parts. Oh!

l'accueillante maison — car c'est bien la "Maison" des élèves! — Comme elle est séduisante, avec ses lambris sculptés, sa décoration artistique, ses vastes foyers ouverts, ses meubles confortables et simples. Et comme il doit faire bon vivre ici! Contre la porte d'entrée, à l'intérieur, nos yeux tombent sur le texte de "Freedom," l'enthousiaste et belle poésie de Rabindranath Tagore. Ce poème, ici, est un programme, n'est-il pas vrai? Car, si "la Vérité s'arrête à l'intelligence, le Beau, lui, pénètre jusqu'au cœur!"

Dans l'enclos fleuri

La journée scolaire commence par une promenade par les allées ensoleilles du grand jardin où les fleurs embaument, où les oiseaux jacassent, où les abeilles déjà butinent. Sur leurs commodes paillassons multicolores, les petits se sont paisiblement assis en rond, autour des arbres. Et voici qu'à la cantonnade, le chouer des grandes, chanté à bouches fermées, monte avec des douceurs d'orgues dans l'air frais du matin. Puis, doucement, au pas cadencé d'une procession, le groupe d'adolescentes s'approche et vient s'arrêter au milieu de l'enclos, sous l'arc des glycines, entre deux lilas blancs. Et là, la chanson grave et largement rythmée s'envole soudain vers le ciel pur comme une ardente prière. C'est la vie qui chante sur l'autel de la nature! Quelque chose d'éminément religieux flotte sur ce jardin. Les petits, silencieux, recueillis, écoutent ardemment l'harmonie des voix humaines mêlées aux trilles des oiseaux et aux senteurs de l'air. A chaque caresse de la brise, il neige des pétales sous les pommiers en fleurs!

This man, internationally known as an educator, seemed to forget pedagogy for a time and to become thrilled with the beauty of the setting in which these children spent so much of their waking hours.

XV

ONE reason for the tardy appearance of a chapter devoted to the teachers in this school is that each time I have attempted it I have been overwhelmed at my incompetency to picture those teachers to you as the real, living, vital source of inspiration and power which they were in our community. A school may have beautiful buildings, all the money it wants, the hearty support of its parents and trustees, but the whole-souled, loyal, unified devotion of its teachers is worth more than all these things put together. With that, in spite of any obstacle, a school will succeed.

How to find the right kind of teachers and how to persuade them, in the early years of our school, to leave steady positions of security and come to the little pioneer school was the question. I had no guarantee except my own personal faith in the idea. I found them by scouring the country, visiting in classrooms, talking with teachers about children, and finally by suggesting to a teacher here and there that she ask for a year's leave of absence and come out to us. One came from the New York City public schools, one from the schools of St. Louis, one from Cincinnati, one from the public schools of Newton, Massachusetts, one from Boston, others from no schools at all. Our genius French teacher I found acting as interpreter in a large soap factory. My own guiding principle was to discover, if I could, by talking with them, whether they were inclined to do their own thinking, whether they would tend to be creative, provided conditions were right. In no case during the early years of the school did I consult a teachers' agency, nor did I select teachers because they had taken any prescribed courses in education. This was not because I had not the greatest respect for the fine work which was being done in this line,

but because I wanted above everything else to find a group of teachers free from any preconceived notions, then to place them in a school environment different from anything they had ever known and let them decide what to do with it.

I had much the same theory about teachers that I had about children. I wanted them to feel free to create for themselves the thing they wanted for children. Of course I do not need to tell you that they throve in such an atmosphere, just as the children did. Imagination, such as they had, and the spirit set free produced not a corps of teachers, but a group of individuals in whom the qualities of inventiveness, resourcefulness, creative genius, and the finest kind of leadership came to the front. Each day new discoveries were made and acted upon. The minute a teacher becomes a creative person, her whole attitude toward her work changes. She becomes happy, eager, expectant, looking upon each problem that comes to her as an opportunity. She is not working for somebody else or following some course of study handed down to her from higher authority. She helps make the course of study. Can't you see, too, what this does to her ability to assume responsibility? She begins to care more than does anyone else that this school which she is helping create shall live.

Our teachers were very different, one from the other. That probably was another reason why they made such a splendid faculty group. It seemed, after we had really begun working together, as though the teachers were almost providentially peculiarly fitted, each to her own grade, as though she had been measured for it by the most scientific rule of child study.

The very first teacher whom I found I put in the most important position of all, the first grade, and there she stayed through all the twelve years, holding the key to our adventure and determining its success more than she ever knew. A timid mother, parting with her child for the first time, would be seen entering the first-grade bungalow, clasping her still more timid child as though she could never let her go; then they both seemed to be enveloped by the sympathy and true understanding of this magician with children, and it would be hard to say which became more entirely her slave.

In addition to an elastic talent for mothering, which was inherent, she viewed the world from a child's point of view, both in fact and in fancy. If you stepped into her room at one moment, you might find her hastily transcribing a bit of prose-poetry or a story which a child was confiding to her or helping mix the paints for the doll's bed which Jimmy was making for his sister, or you might be fortunate enough to enter at that magical moment of hushed, momentous silence which came when the children discovered that they could read the pages of their first books, not primers or readers, but real books. The picture I have of this room is one of twenty-five happy, achieving little people, all entirely absorbed in their many kinds of work, almost always two or three mothers sitting by, usually two or three teachers hovering about, and in their midst a teacher going about quietly, giving just the right help to each child, stopping to reassure an anxious mother, explaining briefly some of the work to a puzzled teacher, but above all, through her own deep abiding faith in the ideals of the school and in the children, unconsciously strengthening that faith in us all.

Teachers' hobbies were seized upon and utilized. It goes without saying that a teacher who spends her spare time making fascinating, original toys and marionettes, boats, and tiny automobiles should have a place provided in her own classroom where she can go on with her hobby in school and make it contagious to children who are fortunate enough to live with her.

Such a teacher I found one summer in a

class which I was teaching in the University of Pennsylvania. She had never taught a day in her life. I don't know to this day just what it was that made me decide to capture her at once from a class of sixty teachers. She became one of the finest teachers of children I ever knew.

One of our teachers was her very best self in her little kitchen at home. She had unusual graciousness as a hostess and still rarer ability as a cook. When she came back to school in the autumn one year, she found annexed to her classroom a tiny kitchen, ready to be equipped by the children under the leadership of a person who loved to make a kitchen attractive. Do you think the little girls of the fifth-grade class will ever forget the introduction they had to the mysteries and the real art of cooking and being hostesses?

Another one of our teachers came to us from the Kindergarten Training School. She came in as an assistant in kindergarten, and how she throve in our atmosphere. She finally, after teaching several primary grades, found herself in our second grade. We found her as talented as she was modest and unassuming. It was she who from the beginning was always seated at the piano when we entered Chapel in the morning. To my knowledge she never refused to play anything which anyone of us ever suggested singing. Hers was indeed a winning personality, and she was simply indispensable to the school. There was no sort of arts and crafts work which she would not attempt with the children, from making attractive benches and tables for the classroom to making all the stage scenery and costumes for any kind of play. She was always on hand, ready and overjoyed to help anybody, always with self-effacement and complete self-sacrifice. She herself was exceedingly original and therefore welcomed anything from the children which tended to be original, especially if it had in it at the same time an element of beauty.

From the very outset our teachers' meetings were a very prominent factor in the development of the school. There were so many thrilling experiences to tell each other about that we finally decided to send the school children home at noon every Wednesday, have lunch together, and talk everything over. On the first Wednesday of every month we had a meeting which lasted most of the afternoon. They were literally teachers' meetings and not principal's meetings. One day in summer I was sitting at a table eating lunch near the University of Pennsylvania, where I had been giving some courses, when I heard a familiar voice at the next table say, "Oh, our teachers' meetings are the most interesting and inspiring meetings in the world," and I heard her go on enthusiastically in words I could not catch, holding the absorbed attention of a group of men and women for at least twenty minutes, apparently describing the kind of meetings we had. When I heard her say, "We wouldn't miss one for anything," you may imagine what such an attitude signified and what it meant to the school.

It was this teacher, an entirely different type from any of the others, upon whom I entirely depended to swing the junior high school group. She was a natural organizer and worker among girls and boys of this adolescent period, with a genius for inspiring them to investigation of every sort. An inveterate research worker herself in the field of geography, she made this subject a study of great industrial problems and even of life itself, inconceivably greater in its scope than the study of even the best textbooks which ever were written.

The enthusiasm about the teachers' meetings was easy to explain. It was a part of an educational adventure we were engaged in. Experiences brought in and discoveries made were a challenge to the best thinking any one of us was capable of doing. During one year, every two weeks all of us as a faculty

observed a class in some subject in our own school. After a good lunch, when nobody felt tired or rushed, we discussed it fearlessly and with good feeling. Often we quarreled heartily, but not over petty details, for those were usually taken care of by the principal in her leisure moments and seldom came in to clutter up the more momentous questions. Sometimes we visited a public school class, giving all our children to our gymnasium teacher for out-of-door play while we were away. Then we brought the public school teacher and the principal back to lunch with us for a discussion of the lesson.

Another way in which we kept alive professionally was by sending our teachers to visit the best schools in the country. The reports which they brought back with them to our teachers' meetings kept us constantly in touch with the best work which was being done elsewhere. Since one of our greatest aims was to serve as a sort of research laboratory for public schools everywhere, it behooved us to keep constantly in very close touch with other schools.

But the fundamental reason why our teachers' meetings were "inspiring" was because a remarkable group of wide-awake teachers, who were entirely absorbed in finding out the real needs of children and trying to meet them, met together in a common interest. I sometimes found it necessary to call their attention to the real goal toward which we were working, when it became temporarily obscured, but for the most part we worked in that respect as an absolute unit.

I can't leave this subject without telling you that every morning when I saw these people coming down the front walk, their faces radiant with anticipatory joy, looking for all the world as though they just couldn't wait to get started in their work, I was ashamed of any moments of doubt I ever entertained about the final success of the school and of its meeting a real need.

XVI

WITH the establishment of our junior high school unit, our plan was complete, except of course that our upper high school included as yet no boys. Can you imagine how it felt after all these years of building, often against terrifically heavy odds, to know that we now could settle down and take account of stock, as it were, check up our work, profit by mistakes, and perfect our school, which now extended from kindergarten to college?

It had been almost a perfect way to build a school, meeting the actual needs of children grade by grade as we came to them. That was undoubtedly one reason why our pupils averaged all the way along more than a year younger than the pupils of other schools. The curriculum was not ready-made but was being made from year to year to meet demands of rapidly growing children who were permitted to go ahead at their own rate of speed, thereby avoiding the great waste of time which is prevalent in elementary education.

Our Primary Village stood in the orchard, its little houses quite literally the homes of the children who lived there. Children's houses they were indeed, each with its own out-of-door classrooms, its shop, with a loft overhead holding every conceivable sort of material which a child could want, each with its own tiny living room built around a fireplace, where one was apt to find a group of children reading poetry or planning the dramatization of a play, each with its own gardens and trellises and woodpile. Little one-story cottages they were and astonishingly inexpensive to build, heated, together with the large dining room, from one central heating plant.

In this village of children its inhabitants were living to their fullest extent. In the large orchard which surrounded them, one

morning I found the kindergarten children working on their miniature village of dry-goods boxes, which they were making into stores, dressmakers' establishments, a station, a post office, etc. A first-grade group some distance away was digging a cave, where they proposed to live as the early cave men. The second-graders were two tribes of Indians, living in wigwams which they had made and wearing costumes which they had decorated. In one of the trees at the other end of the orchard some of the fourth-grade children were tree-dwellers in a house of their own construction.

The third-grade children were actually running the chicken business on a large scale and making money on it. This business incurred the buying of chicken feed, keeping all accounts, taking all the care of the chickens and raising them, finding the market for eggs, etc. Their chicken houses not far away had been built with infinite patience and considerable skill.

The interdependence of these primary families as neighbors made their school living interesting and profitable. These six grades constituted a natural educational unit, and yet at lunch time, at assembly time, and whenever there was an occasion, they came together as members of our big family, which now boasted considerably over two hundred children.

Across the lane lived the junior high school group, using the farm more than the little children did. In the great barn you found them making trapezes and playing in the hay. They took the responsibility for caring for the farm horses and feeding them. Down by the pond they built rafts, and one year they gave *Pinafore* on the banks of the pond. One spring they planned and planted a large vegetable garden, which supplied the summer camp children with all the fresh vegetables they could gather and eat. In the fall, with the farmer, they planted large fields of grain. They planted

potatoes, which they dug in the fall, enough to supply all the potatoes needed for a hundred fifty children for months of lunches. They gathered apples, bushels of them, and sold them. These apples were worth something for the first time in several years because these boys and girls had seen to having the trees sprayed at the right time. Some day I shall write a book about the English and history and world geography and science these children studied which will show the close relationship between their academic work and these meaningful activities, and how much larger a proportion of time was in reality given to the academic work than might appear. But again I say, so many books have been written about subject matter and so many schools are covering academic work so thoroughly and so well that it is my purpose here to stress the importance of environment and a wise use of it as an essential factor in the education of future citizens.

At the end of the drive, you will remember, stood the beautiful home of the former owners, in which now dwelt the high school girls. It was a delight to me just to see them at the end of a period walking down the road in the sunshine to their history classes, which were held at the studio at the entrance of the estate, or over across the fields to the science laboratory, instead of through dark, dusty halls. I liked to see them in all sorts of weather dashing down the hill to our large out-of-door platform for brisk setting-up exercises and then back again to the homey kitchen for hot cocoa and sociability at recess time. I liked to come upon a class in ancient history or a chorus out in the lovely gardens.

In the winter we used our environment to its utmost. A woman who loved the school gave us money to enlarge one of the ponds, and it became a fine skating pond. There were slopes for coasting and skiing, and when the sleighing was good we piled on the farm-

er's big bobsled and went for sleigh rides over the country roads. Always, these girls were busy, responsible, and correspondingly happy.

One day when the girls were given a chance to choose the kind of party they would like above all others to have, they didn't ask for a dance or a movie party. Instead, they invited the boys to come out at the close of school, and immediately upon their arrival they started a game of fox and geese across the fields. They skated and coasted, and finally they all helped get supper in their little stone house.

They had a hilarious time, I know, because I was invited. When it was over they all went home in the big school bus, singing all the way. The boys voted it the "best party they had ever been to."

In twelve years we had grown from the little school of twenty-seven children and four teachers, teaching kindergarten and four grades in the rented cottage, to a school of two hundred twenty children and twenty-seven teachers, ranging from kindergarten to college. We had built or remodeled eleven buildings, including a fine, well-equipped shop and studio and a large dining room. All these, as you know, were ideally set in the midst of a sixty-acre farm.

For my own part I felt as though the school had just begun! The possibilities in such a place, with well-balanced days of Latin, algebra, gardening, "little stone house" responsibilities, and the care of animals, were absolutely unlimited. More than that, we had earned the quiet, peaceful days when the business and the hard struggle of constructing buildings and environment were over, and we could give all our time to the very best use of them all. We could rebuild our curriculum and fit it to meet the needs of children as we found them — not permanently because we hoped to be always rebuilding our curriculum, but wisely, to eliminate waste

and to relate it to real problems of living. We could plan to meet college entrance examinations with no real sacrifice of our educational ideals. The most satisfying and important time of all had arrived

XVII

THEN one day, quite suddenly, my adventure came to an end. A summer came when I fell seriously ill. For months together I went out of the world. Men on the Board who might have saved the situation were abroad. The few trustees left in the city fell into a sort of panic. Finances, which heretofore had never been taken quite seriously enough, now assumed distorted proportions. A weight of insupportable responsibility seemed to fall upon the shoulders of that small group.

School opened. This school, which could easily have gone its accustomed way with its loyal teachers and children to swing it, now for the first time in its history came under the direction of a few members of a Board. Before anyone could tell what had happened, every teacher except two, from the first grade through the junior high school,

had resigned, teachers, most of them, who had done the vigorous pioneer work of the school. When this word was cabled me in France, where I had gone for a half year to recuperate, my resignation of course immediately followed.

There stands out in my mind nothing now of the months of confusion. Only the twelve glorious years remain, during which I was privileged to work with the finest and most loyal group of teachers I have ever met, with splendid, intelligent trustees, with parents who showed unbelievable faith in the school, giving their children under untried and unprecedented conditions, and finally with the children themselves, who will some day exert power in their communities because during their early years they made for themselves clean and honest standards of living to which they will always be courageously loyal.

Will this school live? This question, so insistently asked, is already answered. It is living, not only in this one-place but in many.

Absolutely nothing can kill the idea which came to life in the little cottage so many years ago and which grew so persistently during those twelve creative years. The gracious colonial home with its spreading lawns, its clustering bungalows, is gone. The far reaching elms, the Christmas tree are but beautiful memories. Yet the brick buildings which usurped their places were powerless to thwart the idea which gathered strength until it sought expansion in its farm home. So the gust of misunderstanding which disturbed it there could not touch its intrinsic spirit.

Where and how the school will live to its fullest power no one knows. The greater number of its pioneer teachers are now in supervisory positions, recreating for other children and other teachers their experience.

Again, however, my faith is in the children. They who built the school and lived in it throughout those busy, happy years will demand for their own children an education no

less stimulating, no less rich in opportunities for meaningful experiences, than was their own. To the children, then, may safely be entrusted the enlarged and perfected fulfillment of an adventure which is as unending and as expanding as life.